Thinking of...

Driving Microsoft Dynamics CRM Online from Trial to Subscription in 30 Days or Less?

Ask the Smart Questions

By Jim Sheehan & Steve Thompson
Of PowerObjects

Smart Questions™ Philosophy

Smart Questions is built on 4 key pillars, which set it apart from other publishers:

1. *Smart people want Smart Questions not Dumb Answers*
2. *Domain experts are often excluded from authorship, so we are making writing a book simple and painless*
3. *The community has a great deal to contribute to enhance the content*
4. *We donate a percentage of revenue to a charity voted for by the authors and community. It is great marketing, but it is also the right thing to do*

www.Smart-Questions.com

Reviews

"A well written business book for executives who need to quickly get to the key points of CRM implementation. This will help organizations focus on the right things that ultimately help make decisions impacting the cultural change needed to ensure customer relationship management is a success. A must read if an organization has any interest in growth and sees CRM as a vehicle to take them on the journey to make it happen."

Dave Hutchinson, Executive Vice President, Client Profiles

In our experience as a Microsoft Dynamics CRM Online partner, eSavvy has found this book reflects a lot of the practical aspects and questions we encounter every day. It is therefore a valuable resource for customers and partners to get the most from the 30 day trial process.

David Goad, Managing Director, eSavvy (Australia) Pty Ltd.

Whether public cloud, partner hosted, on-premises or a hybrid solution, Microsoft's strength is the choice it offers customers and the partner eco-system that supports this. This book provides the insight and questions that will allow businesses to understand how to take advantage of this choice.

Warren Nolan, General Manager Sales APAC, NewLease Pty Ltd

Smart Questions for Microsoft Dynamics CRM Online is a no-nonsense way to quickly understand how to drive business with customer relationship management in an accelerated manner. For companies interested in getting in the game, here's the playbook.

Kim Smith, Director, Cloud & CRM Partner Strategy, Microsoft Business Solutions, Microsoft Corporation

Author(s)

Jim Sheehan

Jim has been the COO and a partner in PowerObjects since 2001, he joined PowerObjects to define the direction and create growth opportunities for the company.

Jim studied business and finance at the University of St. Thomas and graduated with a degree in finance. He resides in St Paul with his wife and three daughters.

He has worked over the last few years to turn the direction of PowerObjects from an IT consulting firm into a company with a laser focus on Microsoft Dynamics CRM that works daily to solve business problems. The reason he loves CRM is that it not only gives him a 360 degree view of the customers, but with the integration within PowerObjects he has a 360 degree view into all the areas of the company: sales, delivery, and operations.

Steve Thompson

Talk to Steve for a quick minute and you will be clear that his passion is to help customers realize the benefits of an investment in Microsoft Dynamics CRM to help their organizations succeed.

Steve knows Microsoft Dynamics CRM inside and out and has been working with the solution since before version 1.0 even launched. Having worked with hundreds of organizations large and small over the course of his 17+ years in business technology, Steve has a broad knowledge of various business models and processes as well as the issues and challenges many organizations face in defining and refining those processes.

As VP of Sales Steve leads a team of experienced professionals who focus on solid solution selling, building successful partnerships with customers and most importantly making it their job to truly understand and add value to a customer's organization. Under Steve's leadership PowerObjects' business development team consistently scores very high on the customer satisfaction measures that are embedded in every step of our proven process. The result has been record numbers of satisfied new customers and significant growth year over year for PowerObjects.

Prior to joining PowerObjects in 2008, Steve helped build and lead long-time accounting and business software publisher Red Wing Software. Steve also did a tour in business development with well-respected global enterprise software publisher SAP.

Table of Contents

Acknowledgements

Writing a book doesn't just happen when the fingers hit the keyboard. It begins with the assistance of many people that have helped to contribute in one way or another to providing the experiences for the material, the knowledge to accomplish, and the generosity of time. There are too many to mention individually but we'd like to thank them all for their help and support.

- To the past, present and future PowerObjects team that has worked diligently to help us achieve what we have. Your contributions are immeasurable and this book would not have been possible without your passion.
- To Kim Smith for her time and efforts in providing the Foreword for this book and for garnering the additional support to make this book come alive.
- To those that graced us with insightful reviews and helped to provide supportive feedback.
- To our customers who are our reason for loving what we do and provide us with the motivation to keep doing it.
- To our friends and families for their tolerance of our schedules, understanding of our work, and putting up with all of the initials in our vocabulary.

Foreword

The Move to the Cloud

Over the last few years more and more businesses have begun to move key applications and services to the cloud. At Microsoft, we are making tremendous investments in all of our products to ensure that our customers and partners around the world can embrace cloud computing in the right way for their business – one that allows them to drive higher productivity, deliver more agility, and lower their operating costs.

Microsoft Dynamics CRM has a global track record of delivering world-class customer relationship management systems for large organizations, midsized companies, and small businesses. Microsoft Dynamics CRM Online further extends Microsoft's position as technology leader in cloud services and provides a powerful platform for businesses to drive growth through better and deeper customer relationships and insight.

As companies assess their technology deployment options across on-premises and cloud-based models, these options represent opportunity and risk. With the huge potential that comes implementing a world-class CRM system, it is critical to make the right choices for the right usage scenarios and business needs instead of forcing a decision to implement a solution that just doesn't fit a business' short-term or long-term needs. It is important when evaluating cloud-based CRM to understand what makes sense (and what doesn't) and how to quickly and effectively provide value to new and existing customers in an impactful way that drives long term, trusted relationships.

This guide provides quick and concise guidance for customers and partners to better understand how decisions around CRM are made and how to drive high-value scenarios for Microsoft Dynamics CRM Online in an accelerated manner. It dispels some of the myths around CRM and highlights some of the critical questions to address in implementing a robust and effective CRM experience regardless of business or technology constraints. This information can help you to be more thoughtful, effective, and precise about what you want to offer to the customers and user communities you serve.

I hope you find this information helpful and that it advances your understanding and commitment to Microsoft Dynamics CRM during this exciting time.

Sincerely,

Brad Wilson, General Manager, Microsoft Dynamics CRM

Who should read this book?

People like you and me

This book has been designed for anyone that might be interested in implementing Microsoft Dynamics CRM. Although it deals with complicated technical and business processes, it is not a detailed technical guide nor meant to espouse any particular business philosophy.

This book is aimed primarily at businesses that have an interest in deploying a new CRM solution into their business framework, whether large or small, online or on-premises. There is a heavy focus on the benefits Microsoft Dynamics CRM Online. This focus will appeal mainly to small and mid-sized businesses and organizations that may be deploying CRM for the first time, or switching to Microsoft Dynamics CRM from another CRM solution that has failed to adequately address their needs or has reached its beneficial limits.

Microsoft partners will find value in this book by possibly discovering new ways to engage their customers and better understand what questions they are seeking to have answered during their consultations with you. It is aimed at generating fruitful discussions both internally within the business seeking the implementation, and externally between the business and their chosen partners.

This book is intended to be a catalyst for action aimed at a range of people inside and outside the organization. Here are just a few and why it is relevant for them.

Chief Executive Officer

As the CEO, you are the one ultimately responsible for making the right decisions. Choosing the right CRM solution that fits with the way you do business is an important decision that can affect your entire organization.

If you have been researching CRM capabilities no doubt you have at least narrowed your choices down to a very short list. It is not surprising that Microsoft Dynamics CRM is on that list. But if you still have any doubts, then this book will hopefully alleviate those and reaffirm your decision.

Understanding the Smart Questions can also help you position your organization to achieve the maximum benefits of utilizing Microsoft Dynamics CRM, as well as provide some insight into what those maximum benefits are.

Understanding the Smart Questions will also help you reap the most immediate benefits from implementing Microsoft Dynamics CRM and help show you how to gain immediate value from your decision.

Chief Financial Officer

You will want to know if Microsoft Dynamics CRM Online is a good financial investment and how your organization will be able to get value from the expenditure. How does it compare with other options? Are we locking ourselves in to something that cannot be changed? How will this affect our cash flow? What will our ROI be? And how soon will we realize our ROI?

While this book will not lay out specific numbers, it will help you calculate and plan how implementing Microsoft Dynamics CRM can affect your financial strategy.

Chief Information Officer

You are responsible for formulating the strategy on how IT will support the overall business strategy. How does implementing a CRM solution change that overall strategy? How will information now flow? Who will be responsible for what? What processes can be automated? And who will be given access to what information?

Some of the information in this book may be relevant in helping you formulate a revamped strategy that incorporates the way CRM processes information. Some of the information can also be helpful in helping you learn how Microsoft Dynamics CRM can be aligned or customized to your current strategy.

Chief Technical Officer

Will you need additional infrastructure or can you eliminate the need for some existing infrastructure? Are you able to support an on-premises application or does an online application fit better with your organization?

This is by no means a technical manual, but it will provide some insights into what support will be needed and how any changing business strategies may impact your area.

Department Heads

If your organization is implementing Microsoft Dynamics CRM primarily to assist with sales efforts, then obviously the Sales Manager will find value in learning more about the capabilities and processes involved. But how will a sales-only implementation impact other departments and areas such as customer service and accounting?

It might be beneficial for department heads to familiarize themselves on these capabilities or processes as well. Perhaps they will get added in to the CRM system soon, or perhaps they have some valuable insights on how to customize specific processes that do impact their departments. All input can be beneficial and this book will help those giving the input be more knowledgeable and able to provide that input.

Key Organization Employees

We mention in the book a few times that it can be valuable to seek input from key organization employees that will be involved in using the CRM solution. Why not seek their input early on in the process and arm them with more of a foundational background for providing input?

Microsoft Partners

You are already experts in the ways of Microsoft Dynamics CRM, and this book will not shed any new light on the software capabilities or benefits. But as mentioned earlier, it may shed some light on new ways to generate discussions surrounding Microsoft Dynamics CRM with your customers.

What kinds of questions are businesses seeking answers to? What is important to their unique situation? How can Microsoft Dynamics CRM be leveraged by them to provide immediate returns and value? What do they have to be aware of during the implementation and design process? This book can be utilized as a companion piece for your offerings and possibly help potential customers ask you the Smart Questions.

Clarification of Terms

Throughout this book there are a number of terms that could have different definitions depending on your viewpoint. To help clarify those instances where a word or term has the potential for more than one meaning, we are including a brief overview of what our intended definitions for these terms should refer to:

Microsoft Dynamics CRM – This term will be used in reference with the entire suite of Microsoft Dynamics CRM and could include the on-premises versions of Microsoft Dynamics CRM, Microsoft Dynamics CRM Online and/or other related products.

Microsoft Dynamics CRM Online – When 'Online' is present, we are specifically referencing the Microsoft hosted version of Microsoft Dynamics CRM.

CRM – We will utilize the generic term 'CRM' when discussing either CRM software in general or referring to CRM software other than Microsoft Dynamics CRM. When speaking specifically of Microsoft Dynamics CRM, it will be referenced specifically in conjunction with a 'Microsoft' identifier.

Customer – Since this book is aimed primarily at businesses who may be considering implementing Microsoft Dynamics CRM into their business, or switching to Microsoft Dynamics CRM from their current CRM solution, 'customer' will predominantly be used to reflect the customers of these businesses.

Microsoft Partner – 'Partner' may sometimes be used to refer to the internal or external partners of businesses, which may include software partners. Microsoft Dynamics CRM features a professional worldwide network of Microsoft Partners that can help with consultation, customization or implementation services. These Microsoft Partners will specifically be referenced with the 'Microsoft' identifier.

How to use this book

This book is intended to be the catalyst for action. We hope that the ideas and examples presented in this book will inspire you to act. So, do whatever you need to do to make this book useful. Use Post-it notes, write on it, rip it apart, or read it quickly in one sitting. Whatever works for you. We hope this becomes your most dog-eared book.

Clever clogs – skip to the questions

Some of you will have a deeper understanding of the background of Microsoft Dynamics CRM, or are already utilizing a CRM solution in your business.

We still recommend reading Chapters 1 through 3 to see if you can relate to some of the issues that we see companies struggling with.

There is also some information specific to Microsoft Dynamics CRM that will be useful, before you skip to the Smart Questions.

Chapter

1

Look Before you Leap

Nothing is more terrible than activity without insight.

Thomas Carlyle (Scottish philosopher, 1795 – 1881)

The Great Myths

D URING conversations with CEO's and CIO's, I frequently hear all of the reasons why companies are either resistant to taking the CRM leap or are unhappy with the investment they've already made into CRM relative to the payback they are seeing. My response is always the same: What are you using now?

I hear responses that range from a variety of competing CRM solutions to "We've got our own way of doing things," which could mean anything but sometimes includes sticky notes. One answer I almost never hear is "Microsoft Dynamics CRM."

There are a multitude of reasons for that and we will discuss many of them in this book. We will also discuss how to avoid falling into traditional CRM pitfalls, how to maximize your CRM investment, how to realize some immediate value for your business or organization and maybe even talk a little about fish.

But for now we will look at some of the myths surrounding CRM in general and some of the reasons why you may be hesitant to take your first steps up toward "the cloud".

Most of the reasons I hear that deal with initial resistance can be classified as 'well-justified myths'. There are plenty of figures and examples out there to validate their concerns, but the truth is all of the reasons I hear most often can easily be overcome.

- **Myth #1:** CRM is expensive or only larger companies have the resources to take advantage of its benefits.
- **Myth #2:** CRM doesn't work and experiences a high rate of failure.
- **Myth #3:** User adoption rates are typically low resulting in inaccurate data.
- **Myth #4:** Calculating ROI on a CRM investment is too complex to determine its real value.

All of these scenarios can be proven as fact to some degree and I have talked with many business owners and executives who have experienced the hardships that many of these stories come from. The truth is Microsoft Dynamics CRM Online has also proven all of these scenarios as false for users that have successfully implemented Microsoft Dynamics CRM solutions into their processes.

Let us examine these myths a little closer to see if we can find out why they are well-justified but can also be proven false.

Myth #1: CRM Requires Large Resources for Entry

To look at this myth, let us examine the scenario of a small manufacturing company that had been resisting the urge to jump on the CRM bandwagon due to the large up-front investment they assumed they would have to make. They were in their early stages of growth, but had tapped into a market that was potentially flooded with potential.

They had competitors that were also aggressively eyeing this burgeoning market who were better funded and quicker out of the gate with regard to implementing technology to help them mine the potential market. The race was on. The company needed a way to organize and prioritize sales leads to reduce already tight margins for their products. Having their sales reps "go down the list" in their effort to mine outlets was meeting with slow success and wasting valuable time and effort on leads that had little chance of panning out.

Due to the struggle, the company was also seeing frequent turnover in their sales staff which exacerbated the problem. New sales reps were duplicating efforts of previous unsuccessful contacts because they did not have access to the history of information on those customers. When sales people left, most of the information accumulated on their active leads usually left with them.

Their IT department was virtually non-existent and served to mainly monitor systems and leap into action whenever there was a problem with the network or individual work stations. Hardly the ideal situation, but the company had a good product, a potentially untapped market and solid leadership behind it. What they lacked was a tool that could put it all together and help them effectively reach and cultivate the promising vein of gold they had surveyed.

When presented with a free 30-day trial of Microsoft Dynamics CRM Online, the company soon realized that many of these obstacles could be quickly overcome.

Some "out-of-the-box" customizations helped them seamlessly integrate Microsoft Dynamics CRM Online into the Outlook-based organization tools they were already using. Where previously, sales reps were slow to get information about current clients' account status or were missing out on new "ripe" opportunities to faster-acting competitors, their sales reps suddenly discovered a wealth of information at their fingertips that efficiently helped them re-evaluate their sales process and identify more strategic targets for their product.

Because Microsoft Dynamics CRM Online did not force the sales reps to jump through additional hoops to utilize the new tool, and was constantly available through the software tools they were already using, the sales reps were more inclined to utilize the new tool. And once they began seeing the benefits of utilizing it, the whole process gained enough velocity to help the company dig down far enough to reach that main vein they had been trying unsuccessfully to reach.

Their lack of a 'real' IT department was overcome by Microsoft Dynamics CRM Online's existence in the cloud. There was no expensive hardware to buy, no expensive ongoing technical support staff to hire, and no need to purchase a suite of expensive software licenses.

With little to no technical expertise at their disposal, the company was able to keep all of their sales reps connected while out in the field and take advantage of the steady flow of information that constantly streamed in anytime a customer contact was made throughout their sales, accounting, and customer service and shipping departments. This proved to be an eye-opening experience for the executive team as well as the employees on the front lines.

Due to the "out-of-the-box" customizations that were able to be done during the trial and evaluation process, the company was able to permanently implement Microsoft Dynamics CRM Online into their business strategy within days and 'hit the ground running' without having to stop and start while changing directions.

In short, by implementing Microsoft Dynamics CRM Online the company was able to address their glaring weaknesses and add a powerful missing piece that fit perfectly into their growth strategy with minimal time, financial or personnel resources available.

The results were staggering.

This scenario has been played out with great frequency for many small companies that never thought they would have the resources to acquire the technological tools that could help them mine the potential they knew existed, but couldn't quite reach.

The combination of a 30-day trial and rapid implementation has been able to solve problems such as this time and time again, proving Myth #1 to be one of the biggest prevailing myths currently surrounding CRM.

Myth #2: CRM has a high rate of failure.

The historical numbers of CRM implementation failure rates cannot be ignored. There are some well-publicized numbers out there that often come up in conversations whenever the topic of

CRM implementations comes up. Taken as a whole and with cursory analysis, they certainly imply that CRM is can be a risky investment and require some kind of leap of faith on behalf of the business or organization looking to implement the technology into their business strategy.

Again, there is some well-justified data available that would seem to back up Myth #2.

From 2001 to 2009, a number of independent research studies determined CRM implementations that were deemed 'unsuccessful' or 'failures' ranged from 18 percent to as high as 70 percent depending on the year the study was conducted and who conducted the study.

Why such a large fluctuation? Did some magic implementation formula appear in 2005 that drove down 'failure' rates to 18 percent according to AMR research from a whopping 70 percent in 2002 according to the Butler Group? Did that magic formula disappear again to drive the 'failure' rate back up to 56 percent in 2007 according to the Economist Intelligence Unit? And what of the 47 percent in 2009 according to Forrester Research?

Those numbers are enough to frighten any thoughtful business from taking the CRM plunge head-first. But before leaping off the 'CRM doesn't work' cliff into the same stagnant waters of continuing to do business without CRM, it is probably wise to dive beneath the surface and check the depth of the water as well as discover if there are any hidden rocks lying about those established failure rates.

While there is no doubt that companies have experienced CRM failures, there are plenty of shallow areas and hidden rocks that can help explain the wide gap in consistent figures associated with the mentioned reports and numerous other studies that have been conducted.

First, the studies were completed by a number of different organizations that each used their own methodology. Some studies may have targeted different research goals. Some studies may have used different definitions of 'success' and 'failure'. The companies that were chosen to participate in each of the varying studies may themselves have had different definitions of 'success' and 'failure'. There may have been different scopes of implementation making for an apples and oranges comparison and a lumping of disproportionately-sized CRM projects into the same pool.

This is not to say that the studies are individually wrong. In fact, there is really no reason to question their results. These and many other studies from established, reputable organizations can be called accurate. But when examining CRM as an option for your business, looking before you leap should encompass more than just determining how high the cliff is. If taken at face value, the widely reported numbers from these reputable studies can form the impression of a rather high cliff.

Other studies, many from the same organizations, also show dramatic spikes in companies that are choosing to implement CRM technology into their business strategy. In fact, many major analysts predict unprecedented growth rates for SaaS applications and cloud computing technology that could see market revenues for these technologies more than triple. Yankee Group revealed that "cloud computing is on the cusp of broad enterprise adoption" in a 2010 report based on their research that showed spikes in companies that viewed cloud computing favorably and "viable" for their enterprises.

So how do we reconcile the apparently low 'success' rates or high 'failure' rates with the apparent freight train of cloud computing, CRM technology and SaaS acceptance rates?

The truth is CRM technology works. The key is in adopting it into your business strategy in a way that produces quantifiable value for the specific needs or your business. As we will discuss throughout the book, implementing CRM into your business is much more than just acquiring access to new software and 'flipping a switch'. It is about adopting a completely new business strategy that will help you keep pace with, and even outpace, your competitors by servicing your customers better than the rest of the pack.

The often overlooked human element of CRM coupled with new technological innovations available from Microsoft Dynamics CRM Online can help reduce any apparent CRM cliff to a zero-entry pool that not only does not require a leap of faith, but greatly reduces the impact of making a CRM splash by allowing you to simply wade into the waters before swimming toward your goals.

Myth #3: Low user adoption rates.

This well-justified myth helps explain some of the numbers behind Myth #2. One of the largest reasons cited for an unsuccessful CRM implementation failure is low user adoption rates. It makes complete sense. If the people who are supposed to be using the technologies do not help drive the technology with the information they are exposed to, the results that are supposed to be produced by that technology can easily veer off-course.

Low user adoption will create data that only allows managers to focus in on so much. As they try to drill down further to mine the pertinent information they need, they find they lose their ability to focus. As fewer users continue to work within the CRM system and resort to their 'old ways' of handling their duties, the data available for the decision makers becomes more blurred.

Data Reduction Systems, a New Jersey based data storage and retrieval solutions business faced this same problem. The company considered the CRM solution they had been using as not living up to their expectations. Their employees were forced to run pipeline reports and obtain other relevant data from outside their Microsoft Office and Outlook-based collaboration system they were already using. The extra hurdles required by their existing CRM solution caused employees to tire of the constant jumping and ultimately resulted in a degradation of the data being entered into the CRM flow.

The reduction in data being entered contributed to a reduction in pertinent information that was available to managers and sales reps to base crucial decisions on.

Convinced that CRM technology was beneficial and could help them achieve their business goals, Data Reduction Systems sought to tackle the user adoption hurdle to help them realize the full value of their CRM investment.

After evaluating Microsoft Dynamics CRM Online and determining that its seamless integration with Outlook, Excel and other Microsoft Office applications would remove the major user adoption obstacles that they were encountering, the company was able to obtain a 100-percent user adoption rate after implementing their new solution.

By choosing a hosted solution with a Microsoft Gold Certified Partner, Data Reduction Systems was able to keep their small IT staff focused on their current development duties for the company and quickly get back on track toward accomplishing other important goals such as accurately planning production and identifying important trends so their sales operation could act appropriately.

They were up and running in seven days with a completely new Microsoft Dynamics CRM solution that integrated their legacy data and improved automated workflow processes that greatly improved the accuracy of the decision-making data being analyzed.

The simplicity of obtaining real-time data just by refreshing an Excel spreadsheet helped to eliminate many of the cumbersome processes that were keeping their previous user adoption rates low. The increased productivity and data accuracy also translated into increased sales figures and overall profitability helping to prove Myth #3 as false and allowing Data Reduction Systems to find quick value on their limited investment.

Myth #4: The ROI on CRM is Difficult to Quantify

Yes. It can be. But there has been plenty of research into specific cases of real-world experiences that have made the benefits clear. And as we saw in the last example, Data Reduction Systems was able to quickly quantify their results and according to analysts from

Nucleus Research who investigated their investment in Microsoft Dynamics CRM, the company was able to achieve payback on their initial investment within six months and achieved a 216-percent ROI due to an overall reduction in technology costs and an overall increase in productivity.

Those are pretty happy numbers.

Calculating ROI on an investment such as CRM must take into account a number of areas that can easily be benchmarked to gauge your company's success with the initiative. Some will materialize immediately while others will become evident a little further out.

Obviously, there is the cost of the software licensing, training, consulting and personnel time to be considered. Cost reductions can come in the form of increases in customer renewal rates, higher (and quicker) sales conversion rates, reductions in IT costs and a more streamlined business process.

Again, according to Nucleus Research, ISS Worldwide, a global facility management company based in Belgium, experienced a 2,266-percent ROI over a three-year period after they implemented Microsoft Dynamics CRM as their solution of choice. Payback on their initial investment was two weeks.

After the release of Microsoft Dynamics CRM 2011, Forrester Research conducted in-depth interviews with a variety of businesses in different industries that were implementing Microsoft Dynamics CRM 2011 into their business strategy. Forrester then compiled their interview results into a 'composite company' to evaluate the total financial impact a typical 2,000-employee company could expect with an initial Microsoft Dynamics CRM deployment of 50 users.

Their research of real-world users found a composite three-year ROI of 243-percent with an average payback of 4.1 months. Some of the benefits cited in the study specific to the Microsoft Dynamics CRM application included:

- Increased sales productivity due to the ease of use of the software and its integration with Outlook. Improved sales reporting and sales forecasting led to a more efficient sales process.
- A better user interface and availability of customer data increased customer service productivity enough to avoid hiring 1.5 full time equivalents for an average 10-person customer service department.
- Lower operation costs were achieved across multiple departments from technical to account management due to process improvements that shortened overall time involvement.
- Sales conversion cycles were accelerated by 50-percent
- Marketing costs were dramatically reduced due to better campaign management benefits
- Reporting automation and improved dashboard abilities translated into further productivity savings each month.
- Customizing the solution to meet requirements unique to individual business processes also resulted in cost savings due to the ease of integration with other business technology systems and application flexibility.

These are of course composite numbers and your mileage may vary depending on what steps you take, but they were derived from a broad spectrum of real-world cases. In the cases mentioned above, there are two things in common that helped these companies achieve the results they did.

1. Microsoft Dynamics CRM was their solution of choice and the companies all realized a quantifiable value from the unique capabilities Microsoft Dynamics CRM provides.

2. They had a business change plan to help ensure user adoption which was led from the top and they executed it well.

Those will be recurring themes throughout the book and the benefits of both cannot be stressed enough. You might get tired of seeing them often, but as you can see, the benefits of both cannot be ignored either.

The Next Step

There are plenty of other myths, justified or not, relating to CRM systems and solutions. We'll discover more throughout the remainder of the book as well as how to determine whether or not they will apply to your particular business.

Besides the human element, which we will also continue to explore, the biggest challenge you will face with incorporating a CRM strategy into your business is finding out how to make it fit. You will need to both adapt the CRM to your business as well as adapt your business to your CRM solution. And technology aside, that can be a challenge. But as we'll see in the next chapter, it's not a challenge that can't successfully be met.

> By using established methodologies that have been proven successful, developing and committing to effective business change, and utilizing the right available resources, you can eliminate the need to leap from a CRM cliff and instead walk gently into its waters by finding what fits.

Look Before you Leap

Chapter 2

Finding What Fits

I don't design clothes, I design dreams.

Ralph Lauren (American designer, 1939 –)

A S we have seen, the technology presented with CRM can be implemented to provide solutions to a wide variety of business problems prevalent in varying sized businesses throughout various industries. The solutions all stem from the same steps, but businesses and organizations all tend to walk differently.

There is no ONE way to walk, or ONE way to leverage the technology benefits of CRM. Finding the RIGHT steps that complement the unique way in which your business or organization walks to find the RIGHT solutions is what it is all about.

Again, there are a number of steps that will help you find the path that fits.

Right Focus

A friend of mine recently returned from a trip "Up North" where he spent a week fishing and reconnecting with the woods. Eager to hear about how it went, we got together soon after he got back so I could hear the requisite tales of the ones that (I am sure) got away.

During our conversation, he pulled up his photo album from the trip and started explaining the pictures.

"You cannot really see it, but there is a moose on the shoreline over there," he said, pointing to a corner of the screen.

"This one is a little blurry, but this fish almost took my arm off," he said another time, pointing at what could have been a rolled-up towel.

Ask any photographer and they will tell you that there is more involved with taking a good photograph than simply 'point and shoot'. Even with advanced autofocus features and automated program settings that help you get the right exposure, it is still up to the photographer to frame the picture correctly and prevent cutting off an important detail (such as a moose, in my friend's case).

Similarly, finding the right way to leverage CRM strategy is not as simple as pointing and shooting. You need to compose your CRM strategy to ensure sharp focus and frame it correctly to produce frame-worthy snapshots of your customers and internal processes.

You need to identify exactly what you want to take a picture of and make sure you have implemented all the right settings if you want to identify the picture that is produced when you 'push the button'.

How does a particular process help automate the business? How is the process done today? How will the process be done tomorrow?

Focus in on specific problems with a telephoto zoom, but do not forget to pull back and look at the wide angle as well. There are lots of compositional opportunities between the landscape and the leaf.

The Right People

We have talked a little about CRM technology. Now let us talk a little about CRM people because ultimately, it is the people who drive the technology that will be responsible for steering that technology along the right route to achieve the focused solutions your business is seeking.

I remember a conversation I had with a sales rep for a widget company. We were on a routine short flight and after the introduction and pleasantry period, we quickly began chatting about the sales process. The sales rep described to me how he had developed his own method of selling widgets with the company he was with and was quite proud of his record.

"I have closed three leads this week, and I have got a pretty good feeling I will have my fourth after this trip," he beamed.

I (of course) brought up the subject of CRM.

"We already use it," he said. "But I do not like using it. That is why I developed my own system."

My plane-mate confided that he did not like the way the CRM his company was using forced him to jump around on his computer. He had to dig for all of the relevant information he needed and preferred instead to simply keep his own processes in place that had been working for him in the past.

That conversation revealed a lot. If you are focused in on listening, most conversations will.

On the subject of CRM technology, it should start with a conversation, both internally and externally with your Microsoft Partners, to objectively analyze the challenges your business is currently experiencing. The conversation should also pan out to view the challenges your business is likely to experience in the future. What is it your business is doing well that can be leveraged and where do your weaknesses lie that need supporting?

There are a host of technological options that can be implemented to help alleviate those challenges. Those options should become clearer during the conversations that take place surrounding the CRM initiative.

Partnering with a CRM expert such as the vast network of Microsoft Partners can help surface the right options quicker and help you more thoroughly examine the challenges you are facing.

Internally, who is driving your CRM bus?

One of the biggest assumptions we see companies make is that implementing CRM is nothing more than an introduction of more technology into the mix. In reality, this could not be further from the truth.

Remember the widget sales rep from the plane? Odds are your business will encounter plenty of people that prefer "their way" to whatever "new way" you ask them to do things and for a variety of reasons.

You have decided to implement CRM to help change the way you do business, whether you realize it or not. Your business needs to change in order for it to work.

You will need to effectively manage people to get them to adopt the change as well as provide the right technological solution to help them adopt.

In the case of the widget sales rep, he conceded that a better integration with his Outlook reservoir would have helped him better paddle his way through the CRM stream. That is a technological hurdle that can easily be removed with Microsoft Dynamics CRM.

The "people" hurdle has to be overcome by people. And even if the CRM system his company was using would have seamlessly integrated with Outlook and other every day programs, There is still no guarantee that particular sales rep would have adopted CRM into 'his' process.

Internal People

You will need strong organizational leadership from within the company to champion the CRM cause. Effective change management is essential and all of the standard rules of change management apply to the people inside your business even though CRM is a software-based initiative.

Employees can and will see a CRM initiative as an opportunity for your business to 'trim the fat'. They will want to protect their 'value' to the company and many will be inherently protective of 'their way' of doing things.

Employees can and will feel de-valued as information silos disappear and are integrated into the flow of CRM.

Employees can and will try to protect 'their' data and try to claim ownership over the knowledge resources they have cultivated.

Change management needs to address all of these issues and more in a way that involves those involved in the process feel like they are contributing to, and being part of, the CRM solution.

Long-defined employee roles will change as will the definitions of those roles. Involving employees in the conversation will go a long way to securing they buy-in to the process, boost adoption rates and help you get more immediate value from your CRM system.

External People

Remember as a business to involve your customers in the process, too. This is, after all, a customer-centric technology. Involving them in the conversation can be an important step in the success of the project as, not only can you glean important information (listen) that can help you sharpen your focus on what processes need the most attention, but they will better be prepared to understand any mis-steps that occur along the way.

Involving your business customers in the conversation can serve to enlist them as partners in the process and let them prepare for the changes as well. They will appreciate the inclusion and you will both reap the benefits in the long run.

Another key conversation to focus on is with your Microsoft Partner. They are, after all, the real CRM people. Make sure when you select the people to help you implement a CRM initiative that they truly are CRM people and not just people who do CRM. There is a big difference.

You want people that live, eat and breathe CRM on a daily basis who are tuned in with the latest developments and have experience in providing the solutions to businesses that have faced some of the same challenges that your business is facing.

A Microsoft Partner will help the dialogue flow both ways and listen to get the most value from the conversations you have. They will be able to help provide the right technology solution to fit your business by understanding more about the people processes involved in your business.

Right Process

You have no doubt heard the old saying about trying to fit a square peg in a round hole. Well, implementing CRM into your business can be like trying to fit thousands of differently shaped pegs into thousands of differently shaped holes. And just to add another layer of difficulty, many of the pieces to this puzzle will be constantly moving and changing shape. It is a complex puzzle, but not one without simple solutions.

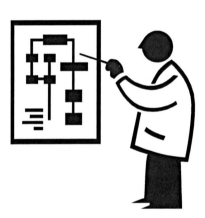

The key is finding the right pieces that fit.

Microsoft Dynamics CRM is designed to offer many pieces that fit well into many business applications, industries, sizes and styles. Part of any CRM implantation is following the right steps that lead to finding the right process that will mesh all of the thousands of different moving parts together.

Your hardware runs on operating systems that contain software and applications that help you with your business processes. Many of your business processes are run by human hardware that employs their own varying set of software and applications to help run your overall business operating system.

All of these parts must seamlessly inter-connect in order provide a clear picture of your business for your customers as well as your employees. Leave out one or two pieces and those holes start to produce a blurry image.

There are many ways to solve a puzzle. You can start with the corners and build from the edges, or assemble isolated portions of the identifiable image and connect those portions together as you build more and larger portions.

There is no ONE process to solve the puzzle. But there is a RIGHT process that you can use to fit CRM to your business.

Do you want to automate your sales force? Do you want to transform your customer service department into a strategic asset? Do you want to gain a full 360-degree view of your customers and be able to determine which customers you should commit more resources to and which ones are draining your resources? Do you want to focus your marketing efforts better to segment, plan and execute your campaigns and more efficiently track your results?

Decide which pieces you want to start with and where you would like to place them.

You will also want to consider the investment you have already made in your current hardware and software systems and decide on a process that protects that investment without adding unnecessary additional expenses.

Do you want to live completely in the cloud? Do you have the capacity and internal resources to support an on-premises solution? Do you prefer a hybrid hosted solution that lets you own the software without having to invest in additional hardware?

Do you need a simple solution for a small team? Or are you looking to build an enterprise system that can be completely customized and scaled up to encompass every aspect of your business?

As we will see in the next chapter, building your strategy around the familiarity and intuitiveness of Microsoft programs such as Office and Outlook, while leveraging the technology behind the Microsoft 'stack', can help you solve the complexities of the CRM puzzle with simple solutions. It will help you find what fits for your business and put you on the next step towards reaching your goals.

Chapter 3

Microsoft Dynamics CRM Online: Stepping Up

Ability is nothing without opportunity.

Napoleon Bonaparte (French Leader, 1769 – 1821)

TAKE a few steps with Microsoft Dynamics CRM Online and you will begin to understand how the value can increase incrementally. It is a foundation piece that offers you the freedom of choice when deciding how to best use it, and implement it, into your business strategy.

Whether you only choose to take those first steps, or continue to climb the CRM staircase as your business grows and expands, it might help to know a little bit more about all of the pieces at your disposal.

Microsoft Dynamics CRM Online

With the release of Microsoft Dynamics CRM Online in January of 2011, Microsoft made a statement that it was "all in" with a push into the cloud. With features such as browser-based and mobile connectivity, real-time dashboards, and seamless integration with the "next generation" Outlook, SharePoint and other cloud services, the cloud has never been more accessible or affordable.

If your business has not joined in the cloud yet, Microsoft Dynamics CRM Online can provide you with the capability to step up into the experience rapidly and efficiently with dynamic results.

At its most basic level, the out-of-the-box features of Microsoft Dynamics CRM Online can provide immediate impacts for your business. The ability to experience the benefits through a 30-day trial and rapidly deploy without the need for internal infrastructure can get your business up and running in the cloud almost instantly.

Some of the most frequently mentioned reasons businesses cite for choosing Microsoft Dynamics CRM Online are:

Value: Side-by-side comparisons of licensing fees, accompanying services and training, deployment, administration, and maintenance reveal a value in savings with Microsoft Dynamics CRM Online for businesses entering the CRM realm or switching from their current solution software.

Productivity: Automated processes and a new level of organizational connectivity boost your business' ability to provide a dynamic experience for your customers and stand out from your competitors.

Familiarity: Microsoft Dynamics CRM integrates seamlessly with the tools you already use such as Outlook and Office providing convenient functionality from right within those applications.

Innovation: Microsoft's history of innovations and industry expertise is well documented and well known. Microsoft Dynamics CRM Online is another example of Microsoft's innovation velocity gained from years of being a leader.

The Cloud: Microsoft Dynamics CRM Online is your express ticket to the cloud and allows your business to take full advantage of the benefits that come with operating from within the new cloud economy. Microsoft invests more than $2 billion dollars each year in cloud infrastructure and can provide the kind of dependability that competitors have yet to achieve. Your path to entry is enhanced with a 30-day trial that lets you customize capabilities to meet your specific needs and see for yourself how rapid joining the cloud can be.

Partner Network: Microsoft Dynamics CRM Online is complemented by one of the world's largest networks of professional partners and third-party application providers that allow you to create the right solution to fit your needs and draw from an incomparable network of experience.

Global Availability: Microsoft Dynamics CRM and Microsoft Dynamics CRM Online combine integrated and localized customization tools in more than 40 languages that allow you to operate, communicate and collaborate on a global basis.

Microsoft Office: You can achieve instant productivity and virtually eliminate the learning curve for your employees with Microsoft Dynamics CRM's seamless integration with your current productivity tools.

Business Insights: Gain real-time, up-to-date business intelligence and data visualization that includes sales forecasting, quotas, customer buying patterns, sales history and more to help increase sales and provide better customer service.

Extended CRM: Why stop with your customers? Microsoft Dynamics CRM gives you the ability to extend the insights and processes that are built-in to your strategic partners, suppliers, contractors and other critical relationships.

Again, this is out-of-the-box functionality that can be rapidly be deployed with customizable features. Did you notice that 'value' was at the top? It's not a ranked list, but the fact is everything included on the above list provides immediate value for your business and contributes to the representative ROI numbers we discussed in the first chapter.

As you can see, Microsoft Dynamics CRM Online provides many pieces to the solution puzzle to help your business succeed. It has the capabilities to serve as a complete picture on its own, but there are more pieces you can use to build upon the foundation it provides to further leverage all of the robust built-in features it offers.

The Microsoft 'Stack'

By leveraging the power of Microsoft's integrated suite of applications, you will have all the pieces you need to create a customizable solution that can fit within any-sized business across nearly any industry and perform a virtually limitless amount of functions.

Microsoft Dynamics CRM Online can serve as a foundation for your ascent into the cloud, but you can easily leverage its robust capabilities by building on the Microsoft 'stack' of applications and technologies to empower your business even more.

Some of the pieces that make up this powerful suite include:

Microsoft Outlook: Most of your team is probably already using this ubiquitous information management tool to help organize tasks, contacts, communications, notes and schedules. Microsoft Dynamics CRM Online lets them gain access to its functionality from right within the screen where they already spend much of their time.

Microsoft Office: There is a reason that someone somewhere on the globe is purchasing Microsoft Office every second. Microsoft's top-selling software suite is a familiar face on most computers. Your employees can interface with Microsoft Dynamics CRM Online in the same way they already use Word, Excel, PowerPoint, OneNote, Outlook, and other familiar Microsoft products greatly accelerating user adoption rates.

Microsoft SQL Server: Microsoft SQL Server is the powerful database behind Microsoft Dynamics CRM and provides the reporting engine and design tools you need to create an unlimited choice of reporting options and customized dashboards. Microsoft Dynamics CRM Online already includes Microsoft SQL Server and the embedded SQL Server Reporting Services and Business Intelligence Design Studio applications as part of the cloud package. For on premises installations, Microsoft SQL Server allows you to build on and extend your applications in the cloud as well as provide support for data warehouses and can be fully integrated with the Microsoft Application Platform.

Microsoft .NET: Microsoft's .NET Framework helps unify a broad range of applications and provides seamless and secure communication that allows developers to build on a consistent programming platform. By utilizing the .NET framework, Microsoft Dynamics CRM can be extended across virtually any business application making it easy for developers to create customized solutions to fit unique business processes and further your ability to climb into the cloud.

Microsoft Office SharePoint: One of the most well received benefits of Microsoft Dynamics CRM Online is the way it integrates with SharePoint. This integration allows team members to easily collaborate and have virtually anywhere access to all relevant documents. Documents can be linked to multiple CRM entities and accessed, worked on and shared with team members anytime, anywhere. Team members and even customers without direct access to Microsoft Dynamics CRM Online can be included in the collaboration or view documents and user-defined security roles help control functional access and track document histories.

Microsoft Lync: Integration of Microsoft Dynamics CRM Online with Microsoft Lync opens a whole world of instant communications and collaborations. With instant messaging, Voice Over IP and Video Conferencing capabilities integrated directly into the CRM system, business can share and discuss documents, presentations, and a host of other materials that allow users to create and alter materials in real-time. It is a virtual conference room.

Microsoft also features a complete suite of IT infrastructure resources including Visual Studio, Exchange, BizTalk Server and System Center that can help you optimize your resources and leverage the integration and compatibility of the complete 'stack'.

Whether you choose to deploy Microsoft Dynamics CRM on-premises and have your own IT department handle customization aspects and process expansion, or venture into the cloud with Microsoft Dynamics CRM Online, you will still be backed by the most reliable, scalable, flexible and knowledgeable CRM solution available.

This capability has proven to provide consistent value for businesses of all size and aspirations.

Stepping Up to xRM

So what if your business aspirations extend farther up the staircase? Microsoft Dynamics CRM Online is your entry portal to do just that. It is also one of the primary reasons why growing businesses who currently employ a CRM solution have been switching to Microsoft Dynamics CRM Online.

As your business grows and you realize the benefits of the Microsoft Dynamics CRM platform, you can leverage the familiar suite of Microsoft technologies and build upon the platform to create xRM applications to match your needs.

What is xRM?

Where 'C' equals 'customer', 'x' can equal virtually anything.

Using the Dynamics CRM platform and integrated Microsoft technologies, you can create business process application that extend beyond the customer relationship, sales, marketing and customer service processes into 'any' relationship and 'any' business process. The scope of what you will be able to accomplish is almost infinite.

xRM can let you more efficiently handle:

- **Vendor Management** – including certification, purchasing and compliance processes.
- **Employee Management** – including new employee and benefits enrollment processes.
- **Prospect Management** – including resume submission, screening and scheduling processes.
- **Project Management** – including RFP and status update processes.
- **Industry Specific Processes** – such as broadcast script creation, disease outbreak tracking, animal lifecycle, grant proposal and tracking environmental compliance processes. Etc., etc., etc., etc., etc...

You get the idea. xRM solutions can encompass virtually any process you need managed with the same robust features as Microsoft Dynamics CRM.

Taking a Step Back

Your business may not quite be ready for that broad of scope of deployment, and a cautionary note should be added here that trying to deploy a broad scope of applications at once will compound the business change management process, increase deployment times and greatly steepen the learning curve.

It is helpful to gain some forward perspective though to see what the view can be like a few steps ahead and should be helpful to know that those capabilities are there when you need them. But let us back up just a bit and examine some of the other reasons Microsoft Dynamics CRM Online can be the right fit with where your business is currently at and how you can take full advantage of the immediate value available in the cloud.

Microsoft Dynamics Sure Step Methodology

We have covered the publicized failure rates that can plague many CRM implementations and talked about some of the reasons why many companies experience disappointing results. One of the processes involved with any Microsoft Dynamics CRM implementation is the utilization of Microsoft Dynamics Sure Step Methodology (Sure Step).

Sure Step is a culmination of successfully field-tested practices that provides a detailed framework to ensure any and all Microsoft Dynamics CRM implementations are successful. This proven methodology ensures consistency and that previously successful implementations can be replicated time after time.

Sure Step lets you implement with confidence and spend more time reaping the benefits of your CRM implementation and less time worrying about the outcome. The outcome is ensured.

The Microsoft Dynamics Sure Step Methodology explicitly defines what responsibilities are done by whom in which order. It defines roles, milestones, processes and project management specifics. It details out the diagnostic, analysis, design, development, deployment and operational phases of the implementation process and can encompass all types of implementations from full scope to rapid deployment, optimization processes and upgrades.

Every Microsoft Certified Gold Partner in the Microsoft Dynamics CRM network is trained on and certified in the Microsoft Dynamics Sure Step Methodology process. This process eliminates a major hurdle to achieving the results you expect and ensuring a successful implementation that allows your business to accelerate its ROI schedule and start accruing value from your investment immediately.

Two Steps Forward

Microsoft has seen unprecedented accelerated growth since it first booted up in 1975. Since the dawn of its humble inception, the company has been propelled by a vision of the future.

Microsoft Dynamics CRM Online is the current culmination of more than 35 years of that forward thinking and serves as another dynamic step in the momentum already achieved with their entry into the CRM realm in 2003. In that time, Microsoft Dynamics CRM has positioned itself well to provide the greatest value available for businesses of all sizes across a wide range of industries now and in the future.

So what of the future? With the speed at which technology is advancing these days, how can you be sure that an investment in CRM now will not fall by the wayside as soon as the next best thing comes along? It is a valid concern. Many CRM systems that have been on the market are already becoming outdated or lack the capabilities to adequately address the future needs of growing businesses.

This is where Microsoft Dynamics CRM is reaching past other CRM applications' terminal velocity and is positioned to ensure its customers keep receiving incremental value well into the future.

Some of the value-added benefits Microsoft Dynamics CRM customers can expect to come include enhanced customer engagement features through social intelligence and business activity feeds that build on the unifying technologies behind SharePoint, Office, Lync and other applications and processes previously mentioned.

Both online and on-premises users will be able to take advantage of twice-yearly updates and accelerated release schedules instead of relying on traditional 2-3 year development cycles of competitors. This will ensure that your business can stay out in front with the latest capabilities available.

Microsoft Dynamics CRM will continue to evolve to bring the latest generations of devices and individual work processes into the fold allowing users to access CRM data anywhere, anytime, from any device and any browser.

That flexibility, agility, adaptability and customizable approach serves as a perfect mirror example for any organization doing business in the Web 2.0 world. It reflects an ability to respond rapidly to changing climates and puts an emphasis on the people involved as much as the technology behind processes. It is a philosophy that fits with the way you do business built on technology that fits with the way you do business. It is always current, always accessible, and always working for you to help cultivate the entire ecosystem in which you do business.

The Power of Choice

When taken as a whole, the array of Microsoft applications and technologies provides your business with a remarkable "Power of Choice."

You can choose to implement in a way that fits perfectly with your business objectives and current capabilities. You can choose to rapidly deploy out-of-the-box customized processes to get immediate results. And you can choose to keep building on the foundation knowing that there is no upper limit in sight for how high you can build.

You can choose a solution that easily fits within your budget objectives and is flexible enough to adapt to your changing financial picture.

You can choose to design tailored processes with the help Microsoft's extensive network of Certified Gold Partners or build your own solutions on the integrated technologies behind Microsoft Dynamics CRM platform.

You can choose to fly freely in the cloud or stay grounded with an on-premises solution - or both.

And you can choose a timeline that fits with your business plan and provides the benefits of rapid deployment for immediate results with long-term scalability that can grow as your business grows.

We hear from our customers that this combination of choice combined with the performance delivered and backed by the people involved provides the greatest value available in the CRM marketplace today.

Driven by the Microsoft vision of the future, the choices available to businesses will only continue to grow, making Microsoft Dynamics CRM the right choice now.

Taking the Right Steps

By now you should have some clarity about some of the steps you will need to take to help leverage the full power of Microsoft Dynamics CRM Online, as well as some of the steps that Microsoft Dynamics CRM Online can help your business take to effect real change in the ability to adapt to a changing marketplace.

We have not discussed a step-by-step approach because every business is unique. Every set of problems require their own solutions and every solution may demand different processes.

But as you continue on to the questions sections, keep in mind that one of the main goals of this book is to help prevent you from taking any missteps during your ascent up to the cloud.

We have seen some stumbling blocks that can exist, hurdles that need to be jumped (or removed), and pitfalls that need to be avoided. We have also seen many helping hands, footholds, and ways to help lift your business up.

Investing in CRM should provide a payback in knowledge - the knowledge to react quicker, the knowledge to conduct business better, and the knowledge grow efficiently. Having the right knowledge drives success and one of the best ways acquire knowledge is to ask the right questions.

You may not be supplied with all of the answers – those will be dependent on who is asking the questions – but they're there, if you look, and if you ask.

So with that in mind, it is time to move forward and start finding out the right steps that fit you and your business. It's time to start asking the Smart Questions.

Chapter 4

Ask the Smart Questions

If I have seen further it is by standing on the shoulders of giants

Isaac Newton (Scientist, 1643 – 1727)

SMART Questions is about giving you valuable insights or "the Smarts". Normally these are only gained through years of painful and costly experience. Whether you already have a general understanding of the subject and need to take it to the next level or are starting from scratch, you need to make sure you ask the Smart Questions. We aim to short circuit that learning process, by providing the expertise of the 'giants' that Isaac Newton referred to.

Not all the questions will necessarily be new or staggeringly insightful. The value you get from the information will clearly vary. It depends on your job role and previous experience. We call this the 3Rs.

The 3 Rs

Some of the questions will be in areas where you know all the answers so they will be **Reinforced** in your mind.

You may have forgotten certain areas so the book will **Remind** you.

And other questions may be things you have never considered and will be **Revealed** to you.

How do you use Smart Questions?

The structure of the questions is set out in Chapter 5, and the questions are in Chapters 6 and 7. The questions are laid out in a series of structured and ordered tables with the questions in one column and the explanation of why it matters alongside. We have also provided a checkbox so that you can mark which questions are relevant to your particular situation.

A quick scan down the first column in the list of questions should give you a general feel of where you are for each question vs. the 3Rs.

At the highest level they are a sanity check or checklist of areas to consider. You can take them with you to meetings or use as the basis of your ITT. Just one question may save you a whole heap of cash or heartache.

In Chapter 8 we have tried to bring the questions to life with some real-life examples.

We trust that you will find real insights. There may be some 'aha' moments. Hopefully not too many sickening, 'head in the hands – what have we done' moments, where you have realized that your company is hopelessly exposed. If you are in that situation, then the questions may help you negotiate yourself back into control.

In this context, probably the most critical role of the questions is that they reveal risks that you had not considered. On the flip side they should also open up your thinking to opportunities that you had not necessarily considered. Balancing the opportunities and the risks, and then agreeing what is realistically achievable is the key to formulating strategy.

The questions could be used in your internal operational meetings to inform or at least prompt the debate. Alternatively they could shape the discussion you have with your vendors, colleagues or even customers to help gain different perspectives.

And finally

Please remember that these questions are NOT intended to be a prescriptive list that must be followed slavishly from beginning to end. It is also inevitable that the list of questions is not exhaustive and we are confident that with the help of the community the list of Smart Questions will grow.

If you want to rephrase a question to improve its context or have identified a question we have missed, then let us know to add to the collective knowledge.

We also understand that not all of the questions will apply to all businesses. However we encourage you to read them all as there may be a nugget of truth that can be adapted to your circumstances.

Above all we do hope that it provides a guide or a pointer to the areas that may be valuable to you and helps with the "3 Rs".

Chapter

A Guide to Success

The ladder of success is best climbed by stepping on the rungs of opportunity.

Ayn Rand (Russian Writer, 1905 – 1982)

CHOOSING to implement Microsoft Dynamics CRM Online will give your business or organization the power to create nearly infinite possibilities. Before you install the engine and turn the keys to your new technology vehicle, taking another look at the reasons you are implementing CRM, what you want to accomplish and how you want to use it will help you maximize its performance and make sure you're on the right road to success.

The questions are divided to provide quick reference for guidance during different phases of the CRM implementation process. Both businesses implementing CRM for their own use and partners performing the implementation process will hopefully find value in at least some of the questions presented here. If any one of the questions can save you from a potential pitfall or spark a new thought process that you might not have considered, then reading through both sections will be time well spent no matter where in the process you are.

Chapter 6: Finding the Right CRM Solution

1. Reasons for Implementation
2. Successful Evaluation

Chapter 7: Successful Implementation

1. Planning for a Successful Implementation
2. Implementation Tips and Tricks

These questions are not intended as a substitute for seeking outside advice and definitely will not answer many of the technical questions you may have. They were designed to serve as a tool for decision makers and those involved in the CRM implementation process that can open internal and external dialogues to better map out and plan for the challenges the lay ahead.

Chapter

Finding the Right CRM Solution

If I had six hours to chop down a tree, I'd spend the first four sharpening the axe.

Abraham Lincoln (US President, 1809 – 1865)

I F you are ready to implement Microsoft Dynamics CRM Online, then you should have already established the answers to many of these questions. Even so, they're worth going over to see what you might have missed or reinforce your decisions.

The questions in this chapter deal with a variety of issues you should consider before undertaking the process of 'going live'.

First, there are questions about why you might be implementing a CRM solution. The reasons why you're implementing CRM should already be clear, but reviewing this section might help you discover new reasons or likewise reinforce your decisions.

Similarly, there are questions for evaluating your CRM system from different angles before you implement it. Even though you might have already gone through the evaluation process and reached the conclusion that Microsoft Dynamics CRM Online is the right fit for your business, reviewing these questions might still help you fine tune your goals.

If nothing else, you should come away from this chapter with a clearer understanding of why Microsoft Dynamics CRM is the right choice and the right fit for your specific needs. There's value in gaining additional confidence in your decision.

Hopefully, you'll discover some questions you haven't thought of that can lead to an even more beneficial experience or lead to more meaningful discussions with the Microsoft partner handling your implementation. The more thorough you think it through and more knowledgeable you are when engaging in conversations with your chosen vendor, the better the overall results will be.

6.1 Reasons for Implementation

So you have tried out Microsoft Dynamics CRM Online and are convinced it is the right choice for your organization. Determining your reasons for implementation will help you better plan your overall implementation strategy. You may already know why you are implementing and what you want to accomplish, but reviewing the reasons and identifying specifics might help you better communicate your goals with team members and your technology partners.

☒	Question	Why this matters
☐	6.1.1 Do I want to improve my planning capabilities?	Easily configured permissions can allow for efficient information distribution and the ability to define territories and teams will help achieve maximum organizational efficiency. Price lists, discounts and unit groups can all be entered into the system to help streamline your offer management.
☐	6.1.2 Do I want to fully automate my lead system?	Microsoft Dynamics CRM can let you automatically assign tasks and leads based on predefined rules, reveal the most promising leads and identify new potential, and help streamline qualification and conversion processes.
☐	6.1.3 Do I want to sharpen sales strategies?	Customer needs can be analyzed on a need-based basis to help you identify gaps and reveal strong opportunities.
☐	6.1.4 Do I want to protect customer continuity?	When salespeople leave or are replaced, a good chunk of important customer information may leave with them. Implementing a CRM system can help you protect important knowledge assets and ensure accumulated data assets are retained by the company.
☐	6.1.5 Do I want to create a 360 degree view of my customers?	Microsoft Dynamics CRM can help you track every contact made with every customer and provide that data to anyone within your organization. All of your customers' history is readily available whenever contact is made providing the ability to make better and faster decisions based on real-time information and a comprehensive historical view.

☒	Question	Why this matters
☐	6.1.6 Do I want to save valuable time resources?	Automated workflows that can follow the unique procedures your business uses can eliminate the need to manually assign tasks and follow up on employees. This can save a compounding amount of time that can better be focused on acquiring, servicing and maintain the personal customer relationship. In addition to automating processes and expediting workflow, Microsoft Dynamics CRM Online can save more time with its seamless integration into Outlook and other frequently used programs such as Excel. There's no switching between applications. It is always working. And a 99.9 percent uptime agreement means you will not lose valuable time waiting for your CRM database to become available so you can access critical information. Taken in aggregate, the cost of time savings increases the more you utilize Microsoft Dynamics CRM's capabilities.
	6.1.7 Do I want to increase collaboration opportunities?	Real-time collaboration capabilities can allow your teams to focus on critical projects and 'meet' from virtually anywhere in the world. Providing your project teams with the ability to centralize resources while having access to real-time changes in status can propel your projects forward. If you can integrate your CRM with familiar and accessible programs such as SharePoint, the collaboration can extend beyond the sometimes limiting internal structure to prospects and current customers to greatly enhance the customer experience.

☒	Question	Why this matters
☐	6.1.8 Do I want to better analyze up-sell and cross-sell opportunities?	The ability to analyze your current customers in-depth can pay dividends on both ends of the profit spectrum. Being able to identify your most lucrative customers, most likely potential customers and valuable customers that may be experiencing difficulties can drive revenues. By examining their full history, your sales team can also be in a better position to offer products or services that might complement the activities your customers are already involved in. Marketing to only those customers with a demonstrable interest or need for the focus of a particular campaign can also save you from a wasted excess in marketing dollars or sales efforts. If you can determine that only 15,000 potential customers are viable candidates, you can better focus your efforts on those customers rather than sending out 50,000 marketing pieces to customers or potential customers that have only a slight chance of responding favorably. There's immense value in 'pruning away the dead branches' and allowing the healthy sprouts to flourish.
☐	6.1.9 Are your existing competitors utilizing CRM to increase their efficiencies?	If your competitors are already using CRM to improve their sales processes, customer service processes, delivery processes or more, your company could find itself lagging in being able to respond and keep pace.

☒	Question	Why this matters
☐	6.1.10 Can you leverage CRM to gain a competitive advantage over your competitors?	If the competitors in your industry haven't yet hopped on the CRM train, can you leverage the power and speed of an online CRM implementation to give you an edge? Competition can be fierce and if you're locked in a tight race as a start-up with other companies trying to enter the same market, utilizing a CRM solution can help provide a little separation. Once you leverage CRM's ability to provide some separation in a critically competitive area or process to gain the advantage, you'll still have the ability to expand that edge to other critical areas. Microsoft Dynamics CRM Online can give you a quick edge with rapid implementation and still allow you the flexibility to 'throttle up' whenever you need.
	6.1.11 Do you want to enhance customer relationships?	In the same way that you can prevent lost opportunities, you can enhance your customer relationships by providing key customer information throughout all of your customer contact points. This not only prevents the 'one hand doesn't know what the other is doing' syndrome, but can also help to more effectively personalize your customer contact experience. Your customers can experience consistency throughout their dealings with your company without having to wait for information to catch up from department to department. Sales reps will be able to provide more knowledgeable and hopefully more helpful solutions, services and products that will also enhance positive customer relationships.

☒	Question	Why this matters
☐	6.1.12 Have you lost business due to lack of insight or mishandling of a customer?	All it takes is one badly mishandled situation to cause a customer to flee. If your customer is met with a steady stream of employees who don't have access to the right information at the right time, your customer can feel like they're not making any progress or gain a view of your company that the right hand doesn't know what the left hand is doing. Have you lost out on opportunities to sell more or better products and services to a customer because you weren't able to recognize their previous buying patterns? Sometimes valuable information can slip through the cracks or go unnoticed when it matters most. A CRM solution can help provide your employees with the proper information to effectively deal with customer inquiries or give your sales reps the knowledge to find the best fits with your customers. Not maximizing your potential sales opportunities can impact your bottom line, but not as bad as losing those potential sales opportunities all together and possibly making it even more difficult to secure additional opportunities from other potential customers.

☒	Question	Why this matters
☐	6.1.13 Do you want to hyper-target marketing efforts?	You can spend a lot of time and money in developing a marketing campaign and trying to achieve a response and conversion rate. There's power in numbers, but there's also higher expenses as well. A CRM solution can help you filter out customers or potential customers that only drain your resources and refocus them on the customers that are most likely to respond. Instead of shining a bright white beacon up in the air in hopes it will attract attention, you can aim your marketing beam through a prism and shine an appropriate color of light that you know specific customers respond to. This can save your company lots of 'wattage'.
☐	6.1.14 Do you want access to more real-time data?	As in the above examples, there are great benefits in the ability to access real-time data when you need it. Playing 'information catch-up' with customers can have serious negative effects that can ripple through your entire organization. A CRM solution can help ensure you have the most up-to-date information available and can be as fast and easy as refreshing the page of the programs you're probably already utilizing to capture and store that information.

☒	Question	Why this matters
☐	6.1.15 Is your current forecasting sometimes inaccurate, hindering cash flow or production timelines?	Again, bad data can negatively skew your projections and result in costly miscalculations or delays in project completion times. A CRM solution can help ensure you can more accurately forecast projected numbers and help provide a firmer target for project completion times. Automated workflows can also help expedite those processes as well as help ensure any glitches or potential logjams are discovered early enough so you can respond effectively and efficiently to keep your budget in check and timeline on track.
☐	6.1.16 Do you have duplicated information stored across a variety of different software applications?	This can cause problems if not all of the duplicate information is being updated consistently across multiple applications. If your employees are accessing the information through different applications, they may be accessing out of date data or missing out on key changes that might have occurred in one department but wasn't updated properly through their method of access. This can also lead to mishandling of customer contacts or make for costly decisions when relying on bad information. A CRM system can ensure all relevant applications are updated simultaneously so your team has the most current and accurate data available and management can make more effective decisions.

☒	Question	Why this matters
☐	6.1.17 Are compiling key reports cumbersome and time consuming?	Do you have to pull data and key indicators from multiple applications and departments? Do you have to dedicate resources to compiling key reports and aggregating the information and data you need? A CRM solution with robust reporting features can let you easily customize the reports you need and present them with a variety of enhancements. This can not only eliminate a cumbersome and time consuming process but will free up dedicated resources to focus on other tasks. Microsoft Dynamics CRM can allow you to look at reports from a variety of perspectives to better get a rounded and fuller picture of internal processes and external activities.
☐	6.1.18 Are you outgrowing your current technology?	As your business expands, rest assured that technology is expanding and advancing as well. It can be resource-intensive trying to keep up with the pace of technology and also expensive to replace technology that no longer has the capacity to effectively help manage your business. Both of these problems can be solved with a CRM solution that provides the flexibility to grow along with your business as well as the ability to stay abreast of the latest technological advancements. Businesses can find great value in utilizing Microsoft Dynamics CRM Online by saving from frequent investment in hardware and software upgrades. You'll always have the best available technology with nearly limitless scalability to match your growth.

☒	Question	Why this matters
☐	6.1.19 Is it difficult for team members to effectively communicate about customers due to their accessibility of information?	If your team members can't access information remotely or have to go through other channels to obtain the information pertinent to the current conversation, the conversation ceases to exist until that information is available. How many phone calls or emails does it currently take for your team members to finish a conversation? Do you frequently encounter, 'I'll get back to you when I get that'? Accessibility to real-time data from virtually anywhere can expedite important customer conversations and help reduce the amount of resources it takes to have that conversation.
☐	6.1.20 Has valuable customer information ever been lost?	Whether it was due to improper backup, mistaken entries, or simply a failure to enter the information, losing important customer information can hurt. Have key employees that have compiled and stored customer information independently left your organization and taken that information with them? A CRM solution can help ensure your employees enter the proper information in the proper places and help ensure you retain all of the information you've collected.

☒	Question	Why this matters
☐	6.1.21 Does your team operate in different 'modes'?	Everyone can have their own 'special' way of doing things and have probably developed some unique 'workarounds' for the processes they're involved in. While this may be beneficial to the individual in the short-term, it can have dramatic negative effects for the organization in the long-term. Employee turnover, disconnected 'modes' and individual preferences can cause information to slip through the cracks or be hoarded. This can create disproportionate access and even eliminate access by other key employees. A CRM solution can help level out the playing field and ensure equal or adequate access is granted to the key information needed to help drive processes.
☐	6.1.22 Are you constantly investing in software upgrades?	The right CRM solution can eliminate the need for constant upgrades and ensure you always have the best available software available at no additional cost.
☐	6.1.23 Is your current IT infrastructure becoming increasingly expensive to maintain?	The right CRM solution can eliminate the expense of major IT infrastructure upgrades, repairs and maintenance allowing you to funnel those dollars into other key areas.

☒	Question	Why this matters
☐	6.1.24 Do you want to increase your business identity awareness?	The advent of social media and mobile apps has changed the consumer game tremendously. A CRM can help track customer experiences and help actively engage customers in ways that keep pace with those advancements. Not only can you better monitor your brand identity and awareness across multiple social media platforms, but you'll better be able to protect your brand identity and increase your awareness through engaging in those platforms as well.
☐	6.1.25 Are your online security systems adequate?	Security is critical in protecting your customers' vital information. Reports of breaches into seemingly well-protected systems by external intruders are becoming more frequent and larger in scope. Is your current security up to the task? Utilizing Microsoft Dynamics CRM Online can greatly improve your security by providing multiple layers that have proven effective against these types of attacks and intrusions. A security breach can be devastating to customer confidence and brand identity. Protecting your accumulated data has never been more critical.

6.2 Successful Evaluation

Once you have solidified your reasons for implementing a CRM solution into your business, you will need to evaluate the software you will be implementing. Microsoft Dynamics CRM Online allows you a full 30-day trial that will let you experience first-hand many of the features and capabilities available. This section can help you identify what to look for during your trial evaluation period and hopefully provide some additional insights into how you intend to utilize those capabilities.

☒	Question	Why this matters
☐	6.2.1 Will I be able to effectively measure ROI?	Measuring ROI after a CRM implementation can be complex and consist of many tangible and intangible benefits. If converting from higher-priced alternatives, the immediate cost savings will be evident. Incremental profit, long-term cost savings, increased operation efficiencies, higher customer retention and improved customer experience can all be factored into the equation. The key is in determining how you will use CRM to improve your different channels and establishing appropriate benchmarks by which to measure specific indicators. Is it priced competitively? While alone this shouldn't be the determining factor, you should try to quantify the overall value. Will you be paying per-computer fees, monthly per-user fees or annual site fees?
☐	6.2.2 How does it help calculate my real business benefits?	Any CRM can crunch data, but delivering the right data to the right people at the right time will be the key to reaping the specific benefits that come from the ability to help you solve specific problems.
☐	6.2.3 Does it provide widespread connectivity?	Will the system be accessible from any connected device or dedicated devices? Does the system guarantee 99.9 percent uptime availability or will you be forced to work around somebody else's best efforts to keep you connected?
☐	6.2.4 Will this help enable accurate budgeting?	Accuracy is paramount to being able to interpret data correctly. Important decisions will hinge on the data your CRM presents. Make sure the systems are in place that will ensure the reliability of the data being presented.

☒	Question	Why this matters
☐	6.2.5 Will it simplify my customer relationships?	In addition to helping your business more easily identify and effectively deal with its customers, CRM should also help improve your customers' experience in dealing with your company. Improve their experience and you will better be able to improve your profitability through higher customer retention and loyalty.
☐	6.2.6 Does it simplify my business processes?	Making your employees' work day easier will help build loyalty, retention and productivity increasing overall profitability.
☐	6.2.7 Is it user friendly?	Stories of abysmal user adoption rates are not hard to find. Gaining user adoption is important to make the CRM function properly. Familiar design and simplicity of navigation will help ensure your users take to the system more rapidly.
☐	6.2.8 Is there built-in flexibility?	Your business has to be able to adapt to current market conditions and unplanned situations on a daily business. Your CRM should not only be able to adapt with you, but provide you with a flexible resource to proactively identify and adapt to those situations before they arrive.
☐	6.2.9 Will I be able to rollback the system?	The ability to rollback applications can help guarantee a smooth workflow in the event any modifications or upgrades produce unexpected consequences.

☒	Question	Why this matters
☐	6.2.10 What specific solutions does it provide straight from the box?	There should be some easily identifiable tasks that can be accomplished without any customization. Do you need quick ability to track a marketing campaign and monitor success while reviewing ownership tasks of various team members? Do you want to shorten your sales cycle, effectively analyze potential sales by territory and identify any neglected leads that may have slipped through your current cracks? Make sure the base CRM capabilities will fit with some of your immediate objectives that you deem most valuable.
☐	6.2.11 What is the customization process?	The ability to provide end users with features such as point-and-click simplicity and drag-and-drop interfaces adds value and saves time without the need for additional programming. Know what will be able to be customized by the user and what larger customizations will need to be accomplished through developers that provide specialized solutions.
☐	6.2.12 Am I choosing a service provider or a business partner?	Determine how much support you will need for your team during and after implementation. Can your vendor supply that support? What type of support can you expect? Will it be in-person, phone, email, or other remote method? A good vendor has a vested interest in seeing your business succeed and not one that is just after a quick sale.

☒	Question	Why this matters
☐	6.2.13 Does it function across my current application platforms?	Seamless integration with widely-used applications such as Outlook and Excel can greatly minimize disruption and maximize adoption times. If you use these programs extensively, your employees are already familiar with the basics of being able to utilize Microsoft Dynamics CRM Online to great effect. It already fits with what they're doing. Attempting to re-invent that process by forcing your employees to adapt to unfamiliar systems can negatively impact your implementation success. The quickest way to begin getting value from your CRM system is to have your employees quickly adopt its usefulness. Make sure your CRM fits into your business and don't try to force your business into fitting around the CRM.
☐	6.2.14 What will the implementation time be?	This will be determined by the degree of customization needed and desired initial results. Implementing CRM can take as little as 48 hours. Implementing it properly to achieve lasting success contains a lot of variables. We will talk more about this process later on, but any implementation should be designed to minimize disruption and maximize the speed of results.
☐	6.2.15 How much am I relying on technology?	As we discussed in Chapter 2, CRM is ultimately a technological tool that will be as effective as the humans who wield it. A strong business plan that consists of identifiable goals and measurable metrics combined with effective leadership will help you get the most from the technology. Your reliance on it should be in direct proportion to your reliance on your team's capabilities.

☒	Question	Why this matters
☐	6.2.16 How well does my provider/vendor /partner understand my business?	Have they dealt with similar business or business processes in the past? What unique problems or processes does your business deal with that will need to be understood by your technology partner?
☐	6.2.17 How often are updates released?	Just as your management team needs up-to-date information to make effective business decisions, your CRM software should provide up-to-date and timely improvements that will allow you to keep pace (and even outpace) your competitors. A typical update cycle of one to two years may not be adequate to keep up with the changing pace of technology. More frequent updates can help ensure you can stay abreast of the latest technology and incorporate that into the way you do business.
☐	6.2.18 What if I want to move my online CRM on-premise or vice versa?	Does the CRM solution offer flexibility in deployment options? If you have already invested in a large IT infrastructure, an on-premise deployment might best utilize those resources. However, if your company wants to take advantage of the full benefits of CRM without having to upgrade their hardware or invest in the infrastructure needed to deploy on-premise, a cloud-based online solution can save substantial time and effort. Also, if you decide on an online employment, what will you need to do to switch to on premise at a later date or vice versa? Will you be able to easily migrate the data if or when you change your deployment model?

☒	Question	Why this matters
☐	6.2.19 What is the financial health of the CRM company?	There are numerous stories of companies purchasing CRM software only to have the companies that provide the software go out of business. A few good indicators of financial stability are how much the company is investing in Research and Development, and what portion of their revenue is allocated to marketing. A large R&D expenditure should indicate the company is serious about developing innovative products and solutions and committing available resources toward moving forward. Where marketing is concerned, the smaller portion of overall revenues the better.
☐	6.2.20 What is the software support level?	How much training is provided? What type of access will be available and when. Who will be providing ongoing support and will it be available through multiple channels? Standard customer service concerns apply.
☐	6.2.21 What is the makeup of the current user base?	Obviously, the more people that are using a product can lend credibility to the value of the product to other businesses and organizations. But just as importantly as how many people are using it, is who is using it. Are their operations similar in size and scope to yours? Have any businesses been able to make notable improvements to their business operations with the product you are considering? Have the specific driving factors that drew you recognize the potential benefits of a CRM solution been successfully addressed within another organization's framework? Search out reviews and responses from other CRM customers to help identify the upsides and any potential pitfalls that other businesses have experienced.

☒	Question	Why this matters
☐	6.2.22 How many concurrent users can the system efficiently handle?	Not all CRM systems are designed the same and you will find variances in the amount of 'load' a CRM system can handle before performance and response time begins to diminish. If you have a smaller business with relatively few users, this may not be a concern. However if you have a large organization that requires a high-capacity for a relatively large amount of users who will be utilizing the system, this might be an important capability to note.
☐	6.2.23 What is the long-term outlook for the CRM software?	Where has the CRM solution come from and where is it going in the future? What type of updates can you expect if you tie your business to a particular software solution and how will that impact your business? In addition to a stable financial outlook you will want to evaluate what type of innovations and 'velocity' is coming out of the Research and Development arena. Can the software history be seen as responsive to market needs? What has the pace of improvements been and what is the anticipated roll-out schedule of future versions? Does the overall strategy mesh well with how you currently do business or how you anticipate doing business in the future? Your CRM software should be able to adapt as often as you adapt your business to meet changing market demands and be flexible enough to adjust with any strategy adjustments you feel are necessary when you feel they are necessary.

☒	Question	Why this matters
☐	6.2.24 What are the reporting capabilities?	Does the CRM solution provide scheduled reports? What kind of flexibility in reporting can you leverage? Your CRM solution should be able to get the right information to the right people at the right time to help your team make the best decisions with the most accurate and up-to-date data available. Can you create a range of visual reports in addition to raw data? How easy is it to generate, share and even refresh the data contained in the report? The greater flexibility and capability in a CRM solution's reporting abilities, the easier it will be to mesh with your business structure and processes.
☐	6.2.25 Is it compatible with my business structure?	Implementing a CRM solution will undoubtedly change many of your business processes, but you should not have to change your business processes to fit your CRM solution. A CRM solution should enhance the way you do business, build on the processes that helped you get where you are, and allow you the flexibility to change your business processes in a way that fits your overall business strategy. If you are forced to alter the way you do business to accommodate the technology behind your CRM solution then you are put in a situation where you are trying to make your business compatible with the solution. That can be a bad gamble at best and a recipe for disaster at worst. After all, it is your business processes and strategy that have played a major role in your success to date. Make sure you do not have to lose any of your strengths for the sole purpose of incorporating a CRM solution into the way you operate.

☒	Question	Why this matters
☐	6.2.26 How definable are the security roles?	How much access to sensitive customer information will you be allowing different employees? Your sales manager will require a deeper level of access than a sales assistant. How customizable is your CRM solution to grant or deny access on different levels without impeding your workflow? Ideally, you should be able to define and assign a broad range of roles with different levels of privileges and access levels within each department. You should also be able associate roles with tasks and be able to easily modify roles or customize roles. Does the system have adequate pre-defined roles built in that can be modified and expanded? This feature can save on implementation time in cases where speed is critical without sacrificing security.
☐	6.2.27 Are there hidden upcharges?	What are you getting with the base package and price that was quoted? Are you getting the full capabilities of the CRM solution or are there different 'editions' that charge you additional fees for increased functionality? Compare what your CRM solution can provide you 'out-of-the-box' and find out how much, if any, you will have to pay to acquire the true functionality that you need. There is a difference between implementing the portions of a CRM solution that will provide the most immediate impact while still being able to build upon its reserve functionality, and paying for only the functionality you need now and having to pay for additional functionality as you build on.

☒	Question	Why this matters
☐	6.2.28 Is data accessible remotely and offline?	Do you have a mobile workforce that needs to access data on the plane? Do they frequently work from home? Can they view critical data on their portable devices when no connection is available? A CRM solution that provides access outside of the normal connection channels can improve your team's productivity and effectiveness while on the road or working remotely.
☐	6.2.29 Is the CRM solution designed to operate intuitively?	There is going to be a learning curve for users with any CRM solution implementation, but you can help limit the extent of that curve by choosing a solution that operates in a way that is familiar with how your employees already work. Again, not all CRM solutions are designed to operate and function the same way, so evaluate how much training time it will take to comfortably navigate around the system. Will your employees have to learn new terminology and get used to a different set of rules than the programs they are currently using? If they do not take easily to the CRM solution it will greatly reduce its overall effectiveness for your business, reduce your ROI and could greatly determine the overall success or failure of the initiative. Do not create any additional roadblocks or provide another set of hurdles for them to jump over that could unnecessarily increase their inherent resistance to change.

Chapter

7

Successful Implementations

A successful man is one who can lay a firm foundation with the bricks others have thrown at him.

David Brinkley (US Journalist, 1920 – 2003)

B Y now you should be feeling pretty confident in the ability of Microsoft Dynamics CRM to provide the solutions you are seeking for your business. We have covered many of the reasons that might have prompted you to explore obtaining a CRM solution or switching out from your current inadequate CRM solution.

This chapter might help convince you further, but it is really

designed to reveal some insight into what it takes to successfully implement a CRM solution into your business and avoid some of the pitfalls that contribute to the 'well-justified' myths we discussed in Chapter 1.

It is not intended as a comprehensive guide – you will still need to develop that on your own or in conjunction with your software provider. Rather, this chapter is designed to generate the discussions that will need to take place to help ensure you are approaching the implementation the right way.

This chapter will also try to reveal some of the best ways you can get immediate value from your CRM implementation and maybe reveal some tips or tricks you have not thought of. We hope it generates fruitful discussions and helps pave the way for you to get the maximum amount of benefit available.

7.1 Planning for a Successful Implementation

As we have discussed throughout the book, there is more to a successful implementation than just flipping a switch. While an online CRM solution can be rapidly installed and get you up and running quickly, there are important questions that need to be answered before you roll out the initiative. This section asks some of the most important questions that some companies may overlook.

☒	Question	Why this matters
☐	7.1.1 Have I identified clear objectives?	You should identify clear-cut objectives for your organizational goals prior designing and implementing CRM into the work flow. You should also identify clear objectives for exactly how CRM will support those goals within the organization. Identifying clearly-defined goals, and effectively communicating those goals internally, is essential in helping ensure successful CRM implementation.
☐	7.1.2 Are my goals measurable?	Some goals may be intangible, but you need to determine measurable goals that can easily be monitored to help realize quicker ROI and help bring long-term goals more closely within reach.
☐	7.1.3 What measurements will I use?	Knowing what you want measured and how you're going to measure it are two different things. Establish defined metrics for each individual goal so you can best gauge your progress and success.
☐	7.1.4 Am I initially over-customizing?	This will depend on your goals. Trying to do too much too soon can lead to greater disruption, increased training, and/or user frustration. In general, the more customization needed from Day 1, the less rapid full implementation will be achieved. You can most often achieve the greatest amount of success by focusing on solving some of your critical problems first. Your everyday users will adopt CRM faster when they can see an especially taxing obstacle or process immediately improved.
☐	7.1.5 Have I tested customized features successfully?	It is a good idea to ensure your customizations are executing and delivering the desired data. Testing the customized features during training before going live could save some headaches.

☒	Question	Why this matters
☐	7.1.6 What incentives am I offering the employees to use the system?	Do you plan to use carrots or sticks? Ideally, your employees will see the value in the system right away and view it as a way to make their lives easier by being able to more efficiently service their customers, whether those customers are external or internal. The need for incentives can be mitigated with effective top-down leadership that effectively promotes CRM as a new business culture and champions the benefits. Implementing the CRM to provide immediate tangible results should be enough incentive with the proper planning.
☐	7.1.7 What will the training process be?	You should identify the scope and depth of training to be provided prior to implementing CRM. Will it consist of online tutorials? Classroom sessions for key users who will then train end users? Or comprehensive training for all people involved.
☐	7.1.8 How can I ensure data accuracy?	Scrubbing data and creating a standardized database during the migration process will be an integral part of a successful implementation. You can work with your vendor to formulate the best plan to handle this.

☒	Question	Why this matters
☐	7.1.9 Have I properly aligned business operations across different departments?	Unless you can reconcile inherent discrepancies that can exist between the different departments the CRM will be deployed to, you'll experience a difficult process. Different cultures and processes can become ingrained within different internal departments even though they may share the same larger business culture. Many times, these contradictory mind-sets can be exposed during a poorly-planned CRM implementation. Proactively aligning the processes to fit cohesively within the CRM system will help cushion the deployment for all areas involved.
☐	7.1.10 Have I documented expected business practices to reflect new operating procedures?	Sales people can be accustomed to converting sales leads to customers in varying ways. A CRM system workflow achieves its greatest potency when processes can be consistently translated in the same way. By not documenting your expected practices with regard to CRM, you are leaving the door open for ambiguity with regard to usage which can cause larger reliability problems with data down the road.
☐	7.1.11 Am I planning properly to prevent project scope creep?	Scope creep is easy to identify once the budget is exceeded or established timelines fall by the wayside. Having a pre-defined plan for how to handle incidents that arise will help limit the ballooning scope of the project. Setting defined benchmarks and acceptable parameters before the process spirals out of control will help meet your pre-determined budget and timeline goals.

☒	Question	Why this matters
☐	7.1.12 Do my 'wants' achieve my desired outcomes?	It is easy to get caught up with all the bells and whistles at your disposal. Make sure you are implementing initially based on need and not want. Microsoft Dynamics CRM is capable of supplying most anything you want, but concentrating your efforts to achieve immediate critical goals will provide the biggest initial positive impact.
☐	7.1.13 Does senior management have available time dedicated?	Executive level sponsorship is critical to any successful CRM implementation. Senior management, whether they are the actual dedicated sponsor or not, will need to be personally involved and available to lead throughout all phases of the CRM initiative.
☐	7.1.14 Who will be the executive level sponsor?	Identify this person or persons early and ensure that they will champion and own the CRM initiative. Organizational change needs to happen even before procedural change begins and often needs to balance maintaining established programs that exist until change occurs. Your executive level sponsor should be tasked with specific responsibilities that are organizationally defined and not just be "handed the keys" to the new car.

☒	Question	Why this matters
☐	7.1.15 What resources will I have to dedicate to the process?	You will need to dedicate some internal resources to ensure success. How much time and how many people need to be dedicated will be determined by the ultimate scope of the CRM initiative. In addition to your executive sponsor, you might want to include a dedicated project manager, a system administrator, department heads and other key users. Depending on your training method, you may also want a training manager or key users to assist in those areas as well. Their roles will vary with regard to different processes, but they should share a common objective of achieving your pre-defined goals and helping to ensure your CRM is eagerly adopted. These resources can also be tasked to carry through with post-implementation guidance and monitoring to ensure your ROI benchmarks are being reached.
☐	7.1.16 Do I have all the relevant data I need?	Some implementations can be hindered by some team members' unwillingness to part with pertinent data they have collected. Many times this is due to team members not wanting to change. They are used to collecting and storing the data themselves and may also feel a sense of protective "ownership" over data they've personally collected. One of the jobs of your executive sponsor and their supporting team will be to extol the benefits of a shared data CRM platform and help them realize the personal benefits that will welcome a different "ownership" model that what they may currently hold.

☒	Question	Why this matters
☐	7.1.17 Should I engage end users from the beginning?	In short, Yes. Identify who some your key users will be and enlist their help in leveraging Microsoft Dynamics CRM's capabilities to best suit their needs. Providing a window that allows your end users to see the benefits of CRM will help to spread the word and build momentum.
☐	7.1.18 Am I viewing CRM departmentally or holistically?	Focusing on improving specific departmental issues and problems will provide benefits for those departments. Focusing on providing holistic benefits across your various channels can provide greater benefits. Providing specific benefits to sales or the call center can produce ripples for other departments that need to be understood.
☐	7.1.19 Am I viewing CRM as a useful tool or a new business strategy?	While Microsoft Dynamic CRM's usefulness as a strategic tool shines bright, you'll achieve the most success if you approach the implementation as a change in overall business strategy. Effectively managing the business change associated with your useful technology will make your CRM shine its brightest.
☐	7.1.20 Am I communicating that CRM is a priority?	Microsoft Dynamics CRM can help your organization provide quality ongoing communication in a timely and relevant manner throughout your customer base. Sometime simply stating that a project is a priority is not enough. An ongoing communication effort that consistently reinforces the priority in a timely and relevant manner will help establish the necessary business changes needed to ensure your implementation is a success.

☒	Question	Why this matters
☐	7.1.21 Are we using a common definition of 'customer' within the organization?	Your IT department's definition of customer will be different than your sales team's definition of customer. Accounting may have a different view than either. Sometimes the differences can be subtle and other times glaring in their practical meaning. Implementing a Customer Relationship Management system will mean different things to different departments. Aligning everyone's definition of what 'customer' means will help alleviate any potential confusion on its purpose.
☐	7.1.22 Have I effectively prioritized my business process changes?	Developing a cohesive CRM strategy might encompass many phases. Prioritizing and defining key performance indicators will better help you align those phases or achieve the maximum return upon initial deployment. What can immediately make an impact? Sometimes it can be as simple as automatically providing your sales team with the ability to pull up prior sales dates to help them better determine when renewals are approaching or that a particularly profitable customer has been neglected for too long. Sometimes it's redesigning a process to streamline an approval or remove an unnecessary step. Whatever you determine your priority to be it should align with the stated goal of your stated CRM strategy and help you move further down the path toward overall process transformation.

☒	Question	Why this matters
☐	7.1.23 What are my 'blackout' periods?	You do not want to roll out a business change program while the senior management team is in the middle of analyzing third quarter results or the sales team is making a final push on a critical campaign. Block out known segments of time that might prevent your CRM implementation from receiving the dedicated attention it will require.
☐	7.1.24 What is our internal marketing strategy?	An internal marketing campaign can prove to be an important business change tool to help employees 'buy in' to the CRM initiative. Different departments might require different 'buy in' marketing strategies. Identify your internal customers and develop strategies to bring them on board early as well as reinforce during and after they 'buy' the product.
☐	7.1.25 What assumptions am I making that need to be true?	It is easy to assume that CRM will find and correct flaws in your business rules or that everyone in your team will immediately take to new processes. But what if those assumptions are wrong? Try to verify any assumptions you have made and honestly evaluate whether they are valid assumptions or not. How will you deal with any assumptions that turn out to be false? An outside view can be valuable in helping to challenge basic assumptions that may be difficult to analyze from inside.

☒	Question	Why this matters
☐	7.1.26 What ripple effects should I expect?	Impacts of implementing a CRM to one area may affect other areas in unexpected ways. They are easy to miss, so plan for some ripples to spread across the pond depending on your drop point. Are implementing CRM in the sales department to provide more productivity and removing certain functions? Will those functions be transferred or eliminated? Will that cause waves in the customer service department who may not be aware of some of the same customer nuances your sales team has come to recognize? How will that impact the overall customer experience? Your CRM partner can help you identify some of the ripples your planned implementation may cause. Identifying as many potential ripples as possible will help limit the waves and position you better to deal with any unexpected fallout.
☐	7.1.27 Where does our critical business knowledge reside?	Recognizing where your critical knowledge stores are will be critical for leveraging the full power of CRM. What are your relational stores of skills and routines that enable you to effectively manage your customer relationships? What are your technological knowledge stores that currently allow you to utilize critical knowledge? Identifying where your critical business knowledge resides can fuel the CRM tank but also help you from inadvertently spilling that fuel in the process.
☐	7.1.28 What decisions do I want my CRM system to handle?	Decide whether you want your CRM to take over processes that can be automated with decision rules or provide relevant information to team members to make better informed decisions.

7.2 Implementation Tips and Tricks

The out-of-the-box functionality of Microsoft Dynamics CRM, rapid deployment capabilities of Microsoft Dynamics CRM Online, intuitive user interface, easy customization, and strategically affordable pricing all offer considerable value. But there are a few things you can do internally to help boost that value and realize even quicker returns. These are just a few ideas, but if you concentrate around the concept of "Think Big, Start Small, Act Fast," there are endless possibilities.

☒	Question	Why this matters
☐	7.2.1 What are my high value processes that need immediate attention?	Microsoft Dynamics CRM can be a powerful tool right out of the box, but it can't fix what's broken. Taking the time to analyze subpar business processes that have been in place, mapping out new solutions, and allowing Microsoft Dynamics CRM to help implement the process change can facilitate gaining rapid value. By engaging key users with solving an important problem that might have been limiting their productivity your organization can help boost user adoption and pave the way for future successes.
☐	7.2.2 What functional area will benefit most from CRM implementation?	By breaking down your long-term goals into a phased approach you can shorten the time involved before users start utilizing your new tool. Will your sales team benefit the most from rapid deployment or the customer service area? Do you have a critical marketing campaign coming down the pipeline that should take precedence? Identify which functional area will benefit most and leverage that short-term success to build momentum toward your long-term goals.
☐	7.2.3 What functional area can I launch to next?	Stick to your phased plan and build on the momentum to keep your users engaged. Act quickly, but act smartly. By deploying in phases you can reduce a potentially complex process down into manageable slices that can provide exponential benefits with each new phase.

☒	Question	Why this matters
☐	7.2.4 What small process can be solved quickly to provide immediate relief?	Focusing on a critical process can provide quick value to the organization, but adding in a 'quick fix' of a minor process known to be particularly annoying or cumbersome for employees can bring great rewards as well. That single small victory can unleash a groundswell of support from end users who will immediately value the solution and can then help you champion its cause.
☐	7.2.5 How can I get people engaged and using the tool as quickly as possible?	Seeking feedback early and often can help fine tune process customizations and win support from the ranks. If your people can notice follow-up actions on their feedback and realize the benefits of their involvement, you'll again earn additional allies to help spread the word.
☐	7.2.6 What will our initial training focus on?	Waiting until deployment to train users on the new software will usually delay its benefits. By focusing on engaging users early on in the process you can better prepare them to hit the ground running once it comes time for deployment. Even if they can't get their hands on the actual product during the trial phase, you can begin communicating aspects of the deployment and generate feedback to begin training them with knowledge. Engage in discussion. Encourage them to ask question. Give them this book to read. Help them understand the bigger picture and how they fit into it by giving them the knowledge to use the tools before opening the tool box.

☒	Question	Why this matters
☐	7.2.7 What type of ongoing training will we utilize?	Initial hands-on training is good, but reinforcing that training with ongoing support is better. It might help to identify some internal stars that can be relied upon to help other users as needed. Peers can often be more readily accessible and easier to learn from and can provide a great internal resource in addition to the external expertise.
☐	7.2.8 What other reinforcement tools can we employ?	Going one step further, if some reinforcement is good, more is better. In addition to making ongoing support available and accessible, schedule additional formal training sessions as needed if only to help hone some processes. And it's okay to have a little fun with a reinforcement strategy to aid in rallying the troops. Throw in some fun perks or 'earned' spiffs along the way.
☐	7.2.9 How can we celebrate our successes?	This can also be viewed as another way to positively reinforce. Celebrating successes can motivate current users to be proactive as well as create a positive anticipation for users in follow-up deployment phases.
☐	7.2.10 How can we encourage proactive usage?	If your sales reps or other users can see immediate benefits through Microsoft Dynamics CRM's intuitive integration with Outlook where they spend the majority of their IT application time, they'll begin seeing it as an ally that can boost their productivity. Once they adopt it as a practical tool, their productivity will translate into quick value for your organization.

Chapter

8

Funny you should say that

Laughter gives us distance. It allows us to step back from an event, deal with it and then move on.

Bob Newhart (Comedian, 1929 -)

T HE purpose of this book is to provide you with the smart questions that will help you find your answers. However sometimes we need to bring these ideas to life with some real world examples.

By seeing the journey that others have taken it can help put into context our own thoughts. So over the pages of this chapter we have included a number of case studies that talk to others experiences and how they have worked their way through to the benefits on the other side.

Case Study: Bomac Vets Plus, Inc.

"With the help of PowerObjects, we have been able to extend Microsoft Dynamics CRM way beyond the initial implementation which has  *allowed us to take our business to the next level. When you have a business that needs to be up and running 24/7, you must have a reliable, efficient and streamlined solution in place. Microsoft Dynamics CRM has become an integral component of how we run our business and we couldn't live without it."*

Punkaj (PJ) Jain, Vice President of E-Commerce   www.ProbioticSmart.com

 Clear skies - life was fine before the Cloud

BOMAC Vets Plus, Inc. is an animal health products manufacturer based in Knapp, Wisconsin, about an hour east of the Twin Cities. They sell many lines of animal products through distributors globally as well as online through its sub-division, *www.ProbioticSmart.com*

 Clouds forming - drivers to migrate

Before implementing Microsoft Dynamics CRM, the company was using an outdated and incompatible system to manage their sales and marketing efforts. They needed a system that would support their marketing efforts and allow them to manage their leads more effectively as well as reorganize client data and track marketing dates more easily.

In addition, the company was looking to expand their business with a new online retail division called www.ProbioticSmart.com to sell to end-users and needed an integrated solution that would help them manage and operate the entire online e-commerce site.

 Cloud cover –our solution/approach

BOMAC Vets Plus chose PowerObjects because of its CRM expertise. The company wanted to move quickly and did not want to add servers or additional software to support the product, so

PowerObject's guidance and expertise. "Overall, PowerObjects has been a great partner to work with and CRM has become an invaluable tool for our company. We are adding more CRM users throughout our organization and look forward to taking advantage of all the functionality that Microsoft Dynamics CRM has to offer," added Highberger.

Case Study: Danos and Curole

*"Before we had to use multiple systems to
access customer and prospect information
and it was difficult and time consuming
for our salespeople to easily access the*
*data they needed. Now, everything is in one place and with the Outlook
integration, we can more effectively manage our customer and prospect
interactions and communication."*

Paul Danos, Executive Vice President   *http://www.danos.com*

 Clear skies - life was fine before the Cloud

Founded in 1947, Danos&Curole is family-owned oilfield services
company with a long history of providing a broad range of services
to the oil and gas industry. Headquartered in Louisiana, with more
than 1,000 employees worldwide, they are committed to providing
excellent service in the areas of construction, fabrication,
production personnel, painting and blasting, and a wide range of
highly skilled consultants.

In order to keep up with growth, better manage customer
relationships and sales opportunities, the company implemented
hosted Microsoft Dynamics CRM.

 Clouds forming - drivers to migrate

As the company was growing, they realized that their existing CRM
solution was not meeting their needs. "Our existing tool was not
flexible and lacked reliable integration to Microsoft Outlook which
we needed to help take our business to the next level," said Paul
Danos, Executive Vice President at Danos&Curole.

 Cloud cover –our solution/approach

After searching for a new solution that would fit their business
needs, Danos felt that hosted Microsoft Dynamics CRM was the
answer. Replacing the existing solution, PowerObjects
implemented hosted Microsoft Dynamics CRM for Danos&Curole
across the entire organization including sales, management, and
operations.

"We looked at many hosted CRM solutions and felt that Microsoft Dynamics CRM and PowerObjects were the best fit. We chose PowerObjects as our partner because of their expertise with CRM and overall disciplined approach to the project. We were really impressed with their ability to understand our business needs and requirements and how CRM could really help get us where we needed to be," he added.

 Sunny spells - the benefits

One of the greatest benefits the company realized with the new solution was the ability for the sales team to access a centralized database of information quickly and easily. "Before we had multiple systems to access customer and prospect information and it was difficult and time consuming for our salespeople to easily access the data they needed. Now, everything is in one place and with the Outlook integration, we can more effectively manage our customer and prospect interactions and communication," Danos said.

One of the key requirements for the company was to have the ability to better forecast sales and manage the sales pipeline with greater intelligence. "Our business is very cyclical, and having the ability to view sales pipeline reports and forecast sales activity quickly has been key to more effectively managing our overall business. Microsoft Dynamics CRM has given us the ability to quickly view and analyze sales data giving us the intelligence to better anticipate and respond to the future changes in our business," he added.

The sales team has also embraced CRM very well. "Compared to our previous system, our salespeople are thrilled with CRM as it has alleviated a lot of headaches and manual processes, allowing them to spend more time selling and less time on administrative tasks," Danos said.

Overall CRM has been a win-win solution for Danos&Curole. "Thanks to PowerObjects and Microsoft Dynamics CRM, we now have a solution that fits our business and it has already proven to be an invaluable tool. We believe the solution has given us a competitive edge in the market and look forward to tapping into all the functionality CRM will bring as we continue to grow," he added.

Case Study: 50Below

"We see the value in what CRM can bring to almost every aspect of our organization. We are working on

eliminating many of our legacy applications which will reduce data entry duplication, and we hope to achieve a 25% increase in efficiency giving us a leg-up on our competition."

Lenny Hubbard, Internal Systems Manager   *http://www.50below.com*

 Clear skies - life was fine before the Cloud

As an internet sales and marketing company, 50 Below designs, develops, maintains, and constantly upgrades large-scale web applications for corporate enterprises with large networks of dealerships, agents/advisors, and franchisees.

Based in Duluth, Minnesota, 50 Below hosts over 100,000 retailer and agent/advisor websites and ecommerce stores. To better administer and manage their existing internal Microsoft Dynamics CRM application, 50 Below looked to PowerObjects to host and manage their CRM application environment and the hardware that supports it.

 Clouds forming - drivers to migrate

As a growing company, 50 Below needed a better way to manage their internal IT support for their on-premises Microsoft Dynamics CRM solution. Focusing most of their IT resources on client projects and services, they found their IT resources very limited in time and experience to adequately manage CRM internally, including the hardware and applications to run CRM as well as Microsoft Exchange.

"We looked at a variety of options and solution providers, but found PowerObjects to have the best CRM experience and knowledge as well as personalized service, which really made the difference," said Lenny Hubbard, Internal Systems Mgr, 50Below.

 Cloud cover –our solution/approach

Taking the IT burden off 50 Below, PowerObjects stepped in and is now hosting and managing CRM and related hardware off site. As part of the service, PowerObjects handles the back-up, monitoring and tuning of Microsoft Dynamics CRM including system upgrades, security patches and roll-ups. "Having PowerObjects handle everything has been a big advantage for us. We don't have to worry about managing our CRM application, keeping up-to-date on the latest technology or dedicate IT resources to it. We know that PowerObjects is taking care of it and we can focus our time supporting other areas of our business," said Hubbard.

As a value-add in working with PowerObjects, 50 Below has taken advantage of PowerObject's PowerPack modules free of charge. These modules, PowerEmail, PowerDashboard, PowerSurvey, PowerView, PowerEdit, and PowerFax, extend and enhance the functionality of CRM. "We have taken advantage of many of these tools including PowerDashboard and PowerView, and they have been a great added bonus and time-saver for our users," he added.

 Sunny spells - the benefits

Hubbard believes the company has realized substantial benefits thanks to PowerObject's expertise and solutions. With the applications being hosted and managed off-site, Hubbard's team has been able to focus on other projects such as extending CRM throughout the entire organization including sales, marketing, customer service, training, and product fulfillment.

"We see the value in what CRM can bring to almost every aspect of our organization and our goal is to have the majority of the 225-employee company using it in some way by the end of 2011," said Hubbard. "In addition, we are working on eliminating many of our legacy applications which will reduce data entry duplication, and we hope to achieve a 25% increase in efficiency giving us a leg-up on our competition." PowerObjects has been a win-win solution for 50 Below. "Working with the PowerObjects team has been great. Their technical knowledge and ability to provide a reliable and robust solution for our company has allowed us to focus on our core IT needs and get more value from our investments. They are a trusted partner and one that we can rely on time and time again," said Hubbard.

Case Study: Yocum Oil

"Before Microsoft Dynamics CRM, our customer and prospect information was disparate and unreliable. Our sales  team didn't have the account-level visibility that they now have. Even if they are on the road, they can login and know exactly what's happening with their customers and have the real-time data they need to sell and service their customers and prospects quickly and easily"

Lauren Carlstrom, Marketing Manage   *http://www.yocumoil.com*

 ### Clear skies - life was fine before the Cloud

Yocum Oil Company, Inc. (Yocum Oil) is a leading supplier of fuel, lubricating oils, gasoline and associated services in the greater Twin Cities area of Minnesota. A family owned company for more than 50 years, Yocum Oil has been serving customers in Minnesota, Wisconsin and Iowa with testing and consulting services, fuel additive packages, and residential and commercial heating oil, fueling, and lubrication products and services and retail convenience centers and car washes. The oil distributor provides 24/7 availability and service support to more than 6,000 commercial and residential customers, with approximately 200 employees operating from multiple locations.

 ### Clouds forming - drivers to migrate

For several years, Yocum Oil used a legacy-based solution along with Excel spreadsheets to manage customer data but really lacked a centralized CRM solution to record customer and prospect interactions, track follow-up activities, manage sales forecasting and reporting, as well as manage and execute marketing programs. As the company continued to grow and expand their business, they determined that their existing legacy system was not meeting their requirements and looked to implementing a more robust CRM solution. Yocum Oil ultimately selected Microsoft Dynamics CRM.

Cloud cover –our solution/approach

Yocum Oil knew that they wanted a cloud vs. on-premises CRM solution to alleviate the need of purchasing new hardware or hiring additional IT resources to manage CRM. "We evaluated several different cloud CRM solutions including Salesforce.com and Oracle, but chose Microsoft Dynamics CRM due to the familiarity our team has working with other Microsoft applications, as well as the skill set PowerObjects brought to the table. We were impressed with PowerObject's professionalism, disciplined approach, and uncanny ability to understand and evaluate our needs. After considering all the options, we found that Microsoft Dynamics CRM would best align with our business needs and goals," said Lauren Carlstrom, Marketing Manager with Yocum Oil.
Within just 60 days, the PowerObjects team implemented and deployed a cloud-based Microsoft Dynamics CRM solution across the entire organization including sales, marketing, operations, finance, and customer service.

 ## Sunny spells - the benefits

"Microsoft Dynamics CRM is a great fit for Yocum Oil. Having a centralized database of customer information has empowered many aspects of our organization," she added.
From a sales perspective, the company has greater insight into customer and prospect information as well as better visibility into the sales pipeline, giving staff and management the sales intelligence they need. "Before Microsoft Dynamics CRM, our customer and prospect information was disparate and unreliable. Our sales team didn't have the account-level visibility that they now have. Even if they are on the road, they can login and know exactly what's happening with their customers and have the real-time data they need to sell and service their customers and prospects quickly and easily," said Carlstrom.

From a marketing standpoint, Carlstrom has experienced great benefits from the CRM solution. The marketing team now has the ability to efficiently run targeted mailing and email campaigns, something that was very time-consuming to execute before. "Using CRM, we can quickly segment the data, pull lists, and execute multi-platform campaigns. Our overall campaign execution time has been reduced by 75%, enabling us to do more marketing in less time and better track the results and ROI," she said.

In addition, because they now have better visibility into customer information, sales, customer service and marketing now have greater ability to reach more contacts, develop better relationships and ultimately keep customer retention rates higher.

Overall, Carlstrom believes Yocum Oil has realized substantial benefits from CRM. "Thanks to PowerObject's guidance and expertise, our staff is much more empowered and productive in their roles. We now have all the information at our fingertips to do our jobs more efficiently allowing us to make better decisions and serve our customers more effectively, ultimately giving us a competitive edge in the market," she added.

Case Study: Windsor Learning

"Before CRM, our staff had trouble accessing the information they needed to do their jobs. Now that we have all of the sales and customer information in one

centralized database that we can access in real-time, we can focus on building new business and servicing our customers even better."

Richard Burrill, CTO   *http://www.pensiondcisions.com*

 ### Clear skies - life was fine before the Cloud

Based in St. Paul, Minnesota, Winsor Learning, Inc. provides instructional reading-based materials and consulting services to PreK-12 school districts and schools across the country. In order to keep up with growth and more effectively support the sales, service and operational components of its business, the company implemented hosted Microsoft Dynamics CRM.

 ### Clouds forming - drivers to migrate

Winsor Learning is a diverse organization with staff located in several locations across the U.S. with some working from remote offices. Before the implementation of Microsoft Dynamics CRM, the sales and service teams would need to login into a web-based Citrix system to access files and forms to process orders and serve its customers. And, for remote users, accessing the Citrix-based system became very slow and difficult to use.

The company was also using ACT!, a contact management system, which did not integrate very well with other applications within the organization, making it difficult to get the information they needed to efficiently run their business. "Both the sales and services organizations had processes in place but it was not easily automated and would sometimes take hours for the data to sync up. We also lacked a way to quickly and easily communicate with one another about what new projects had been won and when and how services would come into play," said Tom Guyer, president of Winsor Learning. "It became apparent that we needed a CRM solution that would help centralize and automate our business from start-to-finish including sales, service, and operations. We looked at other systems but felt Microsoft Dynamics CRM fit our needs the best and would adapt to our business needs in the future," he added.

 ## Cloud cover –our solution/approach

Winsor Learning looked to leading Microsoft Dynamics CRM partner, PowerObjects, to implement a hosted CRM solution. "PowerObjects came in and took the time to understand our needs. They were able to show us how the system would help our business and get us to where we needed to be," said Guyer. "The PowerObjects team was very knowledgeable about CRM and understood the product very well. They were very responsive to our needs and now that we have CRM running and everyone trained on the system, we are very pleased," he added.

 ## Sunny spells - the benefits

One of the greatest benefits the company realized with the new solution was the ability for all the staff, including those working remotely, to access a centralized database of information quickly and easily. "Before CRM, our staff had trouble accessing the information they needed to do their jobs. Now that we have all of the sales and customer information in one centralized database that we can access in real-time, we can focus on building new business and servicing our customers even better," said Guyer. PowerObjects also integrated CRM into Microsoft SharePoint portal, and now the company has the ability to access and share information and data across the organization more easily. "The new CRM system along with the collaboration capabilities of SharePoint has greatly enhanced and improved communication and teamwork between our sales and services organizations," he added. From a sales perspective, Winsor Learning now has the ability to view sales pipeline reports quickly and easily. "Before we'd spend a couple of days gathering the data and now we can pull the report in minutes," said Guyer. "It's made us much more effective in our sales efforts and has allowed us to get the information we needed to quickly analyze our sales performance and make adjustments as needed."

The customer service teams have also improved their ability to capture and report on project status. With hosted Microsoft Dynamics CRM and workflows in place, the company has the visibility and project management capabilities to track projects, assign tasks and check on status at anytime from anywhere. "When our teams would conduct a client review, it used to take up to five days to collect and report on all the information. Now with CRM, we can gather the information we need and prepare the materials in half the time," he added.

Case Study: American Enerpower

"Our business is very document-intensive, and the new CRM system along with the collaboration capabilities of SharePoint has greatly enhanced and improved communication internally as well as with our clients."

Dick Lewis, President   *http://www.americanenerpower.com*

 Clear skies - life was fine before the Cloud

Based in Houston, Texas, American Enerpower provides energy marketing and management consulting services and assists business and residential clients to execute electricity and natural gas contracts with the best price, terms and conditions.

As a very service-oriented company requiring frequent interaction and communication with clients, it needed a more reliable, robust and integrated CRM solution to better respond to client needs on all levels, while having the ability to manage sales and operational components more efficiently.

Using CRM/xRM as a framework for rapid development, PowerObjects implemented hosted Microsoft Dynamics CRM for American Enerpower across the entire organization including management, operations and sales. The CRM solution replaced an out-dated and unreliable proprietary solution that was not meeting their needs.

 Clouds forming - drivers to migrate

American Enerpower was using a propriety solution originally built in Microsoft Visual Basic to track sales activity, client data, and multiple transaction and commission information related to various projects. "Our previous solution was very slow and cumbersome and we continually had issues with its reliability and ability to give us accurate reporting of data," said Dick Lewis, president of American Enerpower. "Being an email-intensive company, we also lacked the ability to integrate Microsoft Outlook with the solution, which made it difficult to track the history of client communication, project status and related information," he added. As the company began taking on additional business, it became apparent that the existing system was not meeting their needs.

 ## Cloud cover –our solution/approach

After searching for a new solution that would fit their unique business needs, Lewis felt that hosted Microsoft Dynamics CRM was the answer. The company looked to leading Microsoft Dynamics Gold Certified Partner, PowerObjects, to implement a hosted CRM solution.

"Our business is unique and we were not able to find a solution that would accommodate all our needs. We chose Microsoft Dynamics CRM because of its reliability, strong platform integration capabilities and one that we could use to recreate many attributes of our old system while adding even more functionality. PowerObjects and Microsoft Dynamics CRM solved our major objective which was to embed a commission calculation capability within CRM that is truly unique and what competitively distinguishes us from our competitors," Lewis said.

The entire implementation of the project was completed within four months. Using the Microsoft Dynamics CRM/xRM platform for development, PowerObjects recreated the proprietary solution that was originally developed in Microsoft Visual Basic, migrated all of the data into one source, developed the workflows and customized the reports. PowerObjects also integrated CRM with Microsoft SharePoint, and now the company has the ability to access and share information across the organization and with clients quickly and easily.

 ## Sunny spells - the benefits

The new CRM solution has made a positive impact on the company. One of the greatest benefits the company realized with the new solution was the ability for all the staff to access a centralized database of information quickly and easily. "Before the implementation, our staff had trouble accessing all the information they needed and now everything is in one centralized database that we can access in real-time.

It has given us the ability to better service our clients and focus on growing our business," said Lewis. PowerObjects also integrated CRM into Microsoft SharePoint, and now the company has the ability to access and share information across the organization more easily. "Our business is very document-intensive, and the new CRM system along with the collaboration capabilities of SharePoint has greatly enhanced and improved communication internally as well as with our clients," he added.

From a sales perspective, the company now has the ability to view client data real-time and track sales from start to finish. "It's made us much more effective in our sales efforts and has allowed us to get the information we need to quickly analyze our sales status and make adjustments as needed," said Lewis. The reliability and stability of the new solution has also brought reassurance to Lewis. "Before we used to continually worry about the stability of the system and the accuracy of our data but now we don't worry about it. PowerObjects did such a great job and has given us the comfort level that everything is running smoothly and correctly.

Lewis believes the company has realized substantial benefits thanks to PowerObject's guidance and expertise. "Overall, the results of the new solution are dramatic. Our organizational efficiency has increased close to 25% to date and it has unquestionably given us a competitive advantage in the marketplace," added Lewis.

Case Study: Cudo

"The main things that really swung me towards selecting CRM Online were the depth and sophistication of the Outlook integration and cloud deployment that also offered us the ability to bring the application in-house or have it hosted by a partner if our business needs change in the future."

Greg Willis, Chief Technology Officer, Cudo
http://www.cudo.com.au

 Clear skies - life was fine before the Cloud

Having entered the rapidly expanding 'group buying' space in 2010, at a time when Australian consumers were embracing the online phenomenon, Cudo has rapidly risen to become one of the largest group-buying sites in Australia.

Because of the great offers it makes available and the wide array of towns and cities it services, Cudo has experienced quick success and subsequent exponential staffing growth; moving from only a handful of staff when it opened to nearly 100 employees...

 Clouds forming - drivers to migrate

Cudo's management knew from the outset that they required the structured business processes that a CRM system could provide.

With a significant investment in its sales force (comprising approximately 50% of the workforce), the main system requirement was to assist management to define and actively manage sales territories and pipeline.

Secondly, the company required a solution that could assist with the management of customer service processes, and thirdly grow to integrate with other business systems.

"We felt it was critical to our business to get a rich CRM platform in place early in the business' life," says Greg Willis.

Cloud cover – our solution/approach

With a preference for a cloud-based solution, and a desire for their CRM to fit with already deployed technologies, Microsoft Dynamics CRM Online became the platform of choice for Cudo.

"We use Microsoft Online for our email and collaboration services, so having a cloud-based CRM was a natural choice for us," said Greg Willis. "The main things that really swung me towards selecting Microsoft Dynamics CRM Online were the depth and sophistication of the Outlook integration and cloud deployment that also offered us the ability to bring the application in-house or have it hosted by a partner if our business needs changed in the future."

Cudo approached the highly experienced CRM consultancy eSavvy to help them design and develop a solution capable of meeting all their requirements.

eSavvy's team of Solution Architects conducted thorough 'discovery' and 'solution blueprint' phases, which allowed the development of a business-to-business and customer service management solution that works with the Cudo business and applications environment.

Solution deployment began during the Microsoft Dynamics CRM Online BETA release, with eSavvy providing consulting around solution design, initial system setup and configuration, solution build and testing, data migration, deployment, license purchasing, training, support, and migration to the live platform when it was released in January 2011.

In fact, eSavvy's initiative in developing the beta system helped make Cudo the first Australian-based Microsoft Dynamics CRM Online client to 'go-live'.

 ## Sunny spells - the benefits

The information and analytics provided by Microsoft Dynamics CRM Online have so far allowed Cudo's senior management to implement strategies that have seen the business grow by 50% month-on-month between December 2010 and May 2011. This rapid growth has occurred because of improvements to business processes and decision making, including:

1) The Sales team moving from a manual process to a solution-supported process. The eSavvy developed workflows and integrated mail-merge functionality allow for 'bookings' to be made with two clicks; saving on average 20-25 minutes per deal.

2) Implementation of dashboards and reports within the Microsoft Dynamics CRM Online solution, which provide Cudo management with real-time data transparency over the health of the sales pipeline – and therefore the health of the business.

3) Provision of an ability for management and marketing to identify which group buying 'offers' perform better within the various cities it operates – allowing Cudo to better target offers to Cudo members.

"CRM is an integral part of our overall business platform. It is already helping us with our original objectives of avoiding territorial confusion within our sales team, and the in-built dashboards provide management with a clear view of the sales pipeline and performance," said Greg Willis.

The online deployment has also provided Cudo with a solution that is completely scalable as the company continues to grow, which provides flexibility for the business, and minimizes infrastructure costs, while providing a built in service level agreement.

It is the versatility and flexibility of the Microsoft Dynamics CRM Online platform that makes all of this possible.

Funny you should say that

Chapter

9

The Final Word

A conclusion is the place where you got tired of thinking.

Albert Bloch (American Artist, 1882 – 1961)

C HOOSING to implement a CRM solution for your business is no small undertaking. As we've seen in the some of the opening chapters as well as the case studies, there are pitfalls to be avoided and numerous benefits to be realized.

Hopefully, this book will have helped you identify (and avoid) any potential pitfalls you may encounter, and helped to provide some quality insights into the numerous benefits that can be realized.

If nothing else, we hoped we answered these four main questions:

Are you ready to implement a CRM solution for your business?

If you have researched the capabilities of CRM and understand the different ways in which it can streamline processes, enable better decision-making abilities, provide a better customer relationship experience, contribute to better bottom-line results, and help provide your business or organization with the tools to better compete, then you'll know if your business is ready to make the leap.

If you have experienced unsatisfactory results from your current CRM solution and are researching the ways in which Microsoft Dynamics CRM can be a better fit for your business, then you should have gained some valuable insight into how you can better incorporate it into your business and how easy it is to 'make the switch'.

Is Microsoft Dynamics CRM the right fit for you?

If you have decided to take the leap into a CRM solution, then you should have gained some valuable insights into how Microsoft Dynamics CRM can accommodate most any situation. Flexibility, scalability, functionality and intuitive ease of use help to set it apart and provide the most adaptable and customizable platform in the arena.

Perhaps the book has removed some imagined barriers or cleared up some misconceptions about CRM. Hopefully you've come to appreciate the value Microsoft Dynamics CRM can afford and how easy it is even for small businesses to reap its rewards.

You should come away confident that Microsoft's velocity in the CRM race is still gaining speed and will continue to provide a stable platform that will keep pace with your changing business needs.

You should also come away knowing that you are dealing with real live people behind the technology, people that have a vested interest in the success of your company and helping you maximize the benefits from your investment.

How will Microsoft Dynamics CRM change your business?

Introducing new or different technologies into your business processes can have unexpected consequences. Hopefully we have helped identify what to watch for, what you can expect, and some of the things that might (and will) change.

Most of all, we hope we have helped identify how to effectively manage any changes that will need to be incorporated and provided you with a helpful resource to ensure those changes go smoothly. Implementing a CRM solution should not force you to radically alter the way you do business. It should fit in comfortably with the way you already do business.

But that does not mean you still will not experience change. You might have to wage some battles to get employees to change or adapt, but hopefully you have gleaned some insights into how to reduce or prevent those battles from happening and gain the employee buy-in that you'll need to realize the full value Microsoft Dynamics CRM affords.

And speaking of employees and customers, just a quick reminder not to forget that CRM is just as much about people as it is about technology. It is about building relationships. The software can be a stable foundation that will help you build those relationships, but those relationships are truly the foundation of your business.

How can you maximize the value contained in Microsoft Dynamics CRM?

Finally, we hope we have included some insights into some other ways you can realize the inherent value contained in Microsoft Dynamics CRM. Getting people engaged and using the tool as quickly as possible is one way, but so is immediately solving critical issues, effectively customizing to fit processes unique to your business, and strategically expanding the built-in functionality to other areas of your business can all provide a quick return.

Start small, get your users engaged, and solve some critical problems immediately. You will find it is easy to build on those initial successes and realize quick payback.

The Final Final Word

You have got a lot of planning to do and nothing will get done as long as you continue reading. So put the book down and create an action plan to begin reaping the benefits of Microsoft Dynamics CRM.

It's not important that every question gets answered. Many of the questions will be answered with additional questions. And that's the whole point of this book. If you can dig through the top layer and start asking the Smart Questions, you'll find a wealth of even smarter questions lying beneath the surface.

There are plenty of resources available to help you dig even deeper and possibly unearth even more questions that can help guide you toward success. A 30-day trial of Microsoft Dynamics CRM Online can certainly help answer many of the questions you might have. There is no substitute for hands-on experience and actually seeing everything we've been talking about in action. So keep the book handy, and refer to it as often as you need. Use it to help guide your discussions and help shape your strategy. But when it is all said and done – as it is now – it is time to take action and begin solving the pieces to your business puzzle. Happy CRMing!

Getting Involved

The Smart Questions community

There may be questions that we should have asked but didn't. Or specific questions which may be relevant to your situation, but not everyone in general. Please let us know at *feedback@Smart-Questions.com*you never know, they may make it into the next edition of the book. That is a key part of the Smart Questions Philosophy.

Send us your feedback

We love feedback. We prefer great reviews, but we'll accept anything that helps take the ideas further. We welcome your comments on this book.

We'd prefer email, as it's easy to answer and saves trees. If the ideas worked for you, we'd love to hear your success stories. Maybe we could turn them into 'Talking Heads'-style video or audio interviews on our website, so others can learn from you. That's one of the reasons why we wrote this book. So talk to us.

feedback@Smart-Questions.com

Got a book you need to write?

Maybe you are a domain expert with knowledge locked up inside you. You'd love to share it and there are people out there desperate for your insights. But you don't think you are an author and don't know where to start. Making it easy for you to write a book is part of the Smart Questions Philosophy.

Let us know about your book idea, and let's see if we can help you get your name in print.

potentialauthor@Smart-Questions.com

Notes pages

Please use these notes pages to capture your thoughts, doodles or random jottings....

Notes pages